OPPOSING
VIEWPOINTS®
SERIES

The Homeless

Other Books of Related Interest:

Opposing Viewpoints Series

Mental Illness

Poverty

Urban America

Current Controversies Series

Mental Health

At Issue Series

How Can the Poor Be Helped?

Is the Gap Between the Rich and Poor Growing?

Is Poverty a Serious Threat?

"Congress shall make no law . . . abridging the freedom of speech, or of the press."

First Amendment to the U.S. Constitution

The basic foundation of our democracy is the First Amendment guarantee of freedom of expression. The Opposing Viewpoints Series is dedicated to the concept of this basic freedom and the idea that it is more important to practice it than to enshrine it.

The Homeless

Louise I. Gerdes, Book Editor

GREENHAVEN PRESS

An imprint of Thomson Gale, a part of The Thomson Corporation

Detroit • New York • San Francisco • New Haven, Conn. • Waterville, Maine • London

Christine Nasso, *Publisher*
Elizabeth Des Chenes, *Managing Editor*

© 2007 Thomson Gale, a part of The Thomson Corporation.

Thomson and Star logo are trademarks and Gale and Greenhaven Press are registered trademarks used herein under license.

For more information, contact:
Greenhaven Press
27500 Drake Rd.
Farmington Hills, MI 48331-3535
Or you can visit our Internet site at http://www.gale.com

Articles in Greenhaven Press anthologies are often edited for length to meet page require-ments. In addition, original titles of these works are changed to clearly present the main thesis and to explicitly indicate the author's opinion. Every effort is made to ensure that Greenhaven Press accurately reflects the original intent of the authors. Every effort has been made to trace the owners of copyrighted material.

Cover photograph reproduced by permission of freephotos.com.

LIBRARY OF CONGRESS CATALOGING-IN-PUBLICATION DATA

The homeless / Louise I. Gerdes, book editor.
    p. cm. -- (Opposing viewpoints)
    Includes bibliographical references and index.
    ISBN-13: 978-0-7377-3654-0 (hardcover)
    ISBN-13: 978-0-7377-3655-7 (pbk.)
    1. Homelessness--United States--Juvenile literature. 2. Homeless persons--United States--Juvenile literature. I. Gerdes, Louise I., 1953-
    HV4505.H654 2007
    362.50973--dc22
    2007006557

ISBN-10: 0-7377-3654-2 (hardcover)
ISBN-10: 0-7377-3655-0 (pbk.)

Printed in the United States of America
10 9 8 7 6 5 4 3 2 1

Contents

Why Consider Opposing Viewpoints?   11

Introduction   14

Chapter 1: Is Homelessness a Serious Problem?

Chapter Preface   19

1. Homelessness Is a Widespread Problem   21
   *National Student Campaign Against
   Hunger & Homelessness*

2. The Problem of Homelessness Is Exaggerated   26
   Mike Rosen

3. Rural Homelessness Is a Serious Problem   30
   Randal C. Archibold

4. Homelessness Is a Serious Problem for Many   37
   U.S. Military Veterans
   National Coalition for Homeless Veterans

5. Homelessness Is a Serious Problem Among   44
   Foster Children
   Kevin Fagan

6. Homelessness Is a Serious Problem for   53
   Abandoned Gay Youths
   Frank Mok

Periodical Bibliography   59

Chapter 2: What Factors Contribute to Homelessness?

Chapter Preface   61

1. Multiple Factors Contribute to Homelessness   63
   National Coalition for the Homeless

2. Substance Abuse Contributes to Homelessness   74
   Diana Mahoney

3. The Mentally Ill Are Vulnerable   **79**
to Homelessness
Harvard Mental Health Letter

4. Domestic Violence Often Leads   **88**
to Homelessness
American Civil Liberties Union Foundation

5. American Wars Create Homelessness   **93**
Coalition for the Homeless

6. Welfare Reform Increases Homelessness   **100**
Francis X. Clines

Periodical Bibliography   **105**

Chapter 3: What Housing Policies Will Benefit the Homeless?

Chapter Preface   **107**

1. Housing Is a Human Right   **110**
René Heybach and Patricia Nix-Hodes

2. Housing Is Not a Human Right   **116**
Michael Tanner

3. Housing Vouchers Benefit Low-Income Families   **119**
Margery Austin Turner

4. Housing Vouchers Do Not Benefit   **129**
Low-Income Families
Howard Husock

5. Permanent Housing Will Reduce   **138**
Chronic Homelessness
Christian Science Monitor

6. Programs That Focus on Chronic   **142**
Homelessness Will Hurt Homeless Families
Gloria M. Guard

Periodical Bibliography   **147**

Chapter 4: What Policies Will Best Reduce Homelessness?

Chapter Preface   149

1. Government Initiatives Can   151
   Reduce Homelessness
   Philip F. Mangano

2. Government Initiatives Will Not   158
   Reduce Homelessness
   John Derbyshire

3. Housing Vouchers Will Help Homeless   164
   Hurricane Katrina Victims
   Bruce Katz and Mark Muro

4. Vouchers Are Inadequate to Help Many   169
   Homeless Hurricane Katrina Victims
   Greg Anrig Jr.

5. People Should Give Money to Panhandlers   174
   Reggie Rivers

6. People Should Not Give Money   178
   to Panhandlers
   Brad Edmonds

Periodical Bibliography   182

For Further Discussion   183

Organizations to Contact   187

Bibliography of Books   193

Index   196

Why Consider Opposing Viewpoints?

> *"The only way in which a human being can make some approach to knowing the whole of a subject is by hearing what can be said about it by persons of every variety of opinion and studying all modes in which it can be looked at by every character of mind. No wise man ever acquired his wisdom in any mode but this."*
>
> *John Stuart Mill*

In our media-intensive culture it is not difficult to find differing opinions. Thousands of newspapers and magazines and dozens of radio and television talk shows resound with differing points of view. The difficulty lies in deciding which opinion to agree with and which "experts" seem the most credible. The more inundated we become with differing opinions and claims, the more essential it is to hone critical reading and thinking skills to evaluate these ideas. Opposing Viewpoints books address this problem directly by presenting stimulating debates that can be used to enhance and teach these skills. The varied opinions contained in each book examine many different aspects of a single issue. While examining these conveniently edited opposing views, readers can develop critical thinking skills such as the ability to compare and contrast authors' credibility, facts, argumentation styles, use of persuasive techniques, and other stylistic tools. In short, the Opposing Viewpoints series is an ideal way to attain the higher-level thinking and reading skills so essential in a culture of diverse and contradictory opinions.

In addition to providing a tool for critical thinking, Opposing Viewpoints books challenge readers to question their own strongly held opinions and assumptions. Most people form their opinions on the basis of upbringing, peer pressure, and personal, cultural, or professional bias. By reading carefully balanced opposing views, readers must directly confront new ideas as well as the opinions of those with whom they disagree. This is not to simplistically argue that everyone who reads opposing views will—or should—change his or her opinion. Instead, the series enhances readers' understanding of their own views by encouraging confrontation with opposing ideas. Careful examination of others' views can lead to the readers' understanding of the logical inconsistencies in their own opinions, perspective on why they hold an opinion, and the consideration of the possibility that their opinion requires further evaluation.

Evaluating Other Opinions

To ensure that this type of examination occurs, Opposing Viewpoints books present all types of opinions. Prominent spokespeople on different sides of each issue as well as well-known professionals from many disciplines challenge the reader. An additional goal of the series is to provide a forum for other, less-known, or even unpopular viewpoints. The opinion of an ordinary person who has had to make the decision to cut off life support from a terminally ill relative, for example, may be just as valuable and provide just as much insight as a medical ethicist's professional opinion. The editors have two additional purposes in including these less-known views. One, the editors encourage readers to respect others' opinions—even when not enhanced by professional credibility. It is only by reading or listening to and objectively evaluating others' ideas that one can determine whether they are worthy of consideration. Two, the inclusion of such viewpoints encourages the important critical thinking skill of objectively evaluating an author's credentials and bias. This evaluation will illuminate an author's reasons for taking a particular stance on an issue and will aid in readers' evaluation of the author's ideas.

It is our hope that these books will give readers a deeper understanding of the issues debated and an appreciation of the complexity of even seemingly simple issues when good and honest people disagree. This awareness is particularly important in a democratic society such as ours in which people enter into public debate to determine the common good. Those with whom one disagrees should not be regarded as enemies but rather as people whose views deserve careful examination and may shed light on one's own.

Thomas Jefferson once said that "difference of opinion leads to inquiry, and inquiry to truth." Jefferson, a broadly educated man, argued that "if a nation expects to be ignorant and free . . . it expects what never was and never will be." As individuals and as a nation, it is imperative that we consider the opinions of others and examine them with skill and discernment. The Opposing Viewpoints series is intended to help readers achieve this goal.

David L. Bender and Bruno Leone,
Founders

Introduction

> *"It will take optimism—and a healthy dose of strength, patience and persistence—to wrestle homelessness from our cities. . . . But these are qualities Americans have in abundance."*
>
> Mel Martinez,
> U.S. Secretary of Housing

A merican policies have always distinguished between the "deserving" and the "undeserving" poor. Indeed, this distinction has, over the years, determined who among the homeless would receive assistance. At the core of the homelessness controversy lie the questions, how should the homeless be defined, and who should be responsible for their care? In the late nineteenth and early twentieth centuries, private charities and local governments helped those whose homelessness was, in the eyes of society, beyond their control. At the time, few considered substance abuse beyond the control of the abuser, and even fewer understood postwar mental illnesses such as post-traumatic stress disorder, although many homeless people suffered from these diseases. Thus widows, orphans, the recently jobless, and those with severe illnesses or physical handicaps received food and shelter. Vagrants, men who appeared able-bodied but who refused to work, received contempt from the community.

These attitudes and policies continued until the 1930s. During the economic collapse known as the Great Depression, however, the number of unemployed grew exponentially, and many Americans became homeless. Homelessness was no longer an isolated problem, the result of local circumstances. Instead, it was widespread, the result of a worldwide economic collapse, and local governments and charities were unable to cope with the enormity of the problem. During the Great Depression the federal government, with the support of a weary citizenry, for the first time assumed a major role in the battle against poverty and homelessness. President Franklin D. Roosevelt's Federal Emergency Relief Administration provided clothing, food, shelter, medical care, and cash to the homeless, and the Works Progress Administration created jobs. These programs were discontinued during World War II when economic production increased, nearly eliminating unemployment. The economic boom continued, and pre-Depression attitudes toward the homeless returned. Local governments and private charity again bore the responsibility of caring for the homeless.

Homelessness reemerged as a national issue in the 1980s. Controversial reports that millions of Americans were homeless, many of whom were families with children, stirred public support for federal action. Homeless activist Mitch Snyder's 1982 report, "Homelessness in America: A Forced March to Nowhere," estimated that 2.2 million Americans were without shelter, and he predicted that this number would reach 3 million by 1983. According to sociology professor Christopher Jencks this figure was treated as a well-established fact, although the source of these numbers was never verified. Those opposed to government assistance disputed Snyder's claims. The public clamored for a solution, however, and challenges to Snyder's figures fell on deaf ears. In 1987 Congress passed the Stewart B. McKinney Homeless Assistance Act, authorizing hundreds of millions of dollars in aid for the homeless.

Despite the McKinney Act's substantial funding to address homelessness, the problem remains, and contemporary analysts question traditional policies. Critics claim that homelessness is more than simply the lack of a home. According to Robert Rector of the conservative Heritage Foundation, homelessness is an "incidental symptom of other more fundamental problems," such as substance abuse or mental illness. Homelessness exists, he argues, "precisely because we have not succeeded in dealing with those other problems." Like-minded analysts assert that funding spent on homeless shelters merely manages the problem. The small percentage of chronic homeless, they argue, consume a large portion of resources yet continue to cycle through the shelter system.

In March 2004 several members of Congress, with strong support from the White House, introduced the Samaritan Initiative. The initiative's goal is to eliminate chronic homelessness by providing permanent housing that would include supportive services needed to address the substance abuse and mental health problems of the chronic homeless. As of January 2007, the bill remained in committee.

Initiative opponents argue that a focus on chronic homelessness is misguided. Policies that focus on such a narrow group neglect the needs of the greater homeless population, particularly families with children, they contend. According to Nan Roman, president of the National Alliance to End Homelessness, "One size does not fit all." The homeless population, she explains, is diverse: 40 percent are families with children, 30 percent are substance abusers, 23 percent are severely mentally ill, 17 percent are employed, and 10 percent are veterans. Programs to end chronic homelessness, she asserts, must not ignore those who need temporary shelter and support services such as job training, transportation, and child care to get back on their feet. These advocates for the homeless argue that homelessness is the result of greater societal wrongs. "We as a Congress need to look at everything that promotes homelessness," declares Representative Julia Carson, "and see what we can do to counteract it." Carson introduced The Bringing America Home Act, a comprehensive homelessness initiative that addresses housing, health, poverty, and civil rights. As of January 2007, this bill also remained in committee.

The debate over how best to define and help the homeless continues. At the core of the controversy is whether the homeless are a narrow population who need specific services or a broad population suffering from more pervasive societal ills. The authors in this volume debate these and other issues concerning the nature and scope of homelessness in the following chapters of *Opposing Viewpoints: The Homeless*: Is Homelessness a Serious Problem? What Factors Contribute to Homelessness? What Housing Policies Will Benefit the Homeless? What Policies Will Best Reduce Homelessness? How these views will define and affect policy in the future remains to be seen.

OPPOSING
VIEWPOINTS®
SERIES

CHAPTER 1

Is Homelessness a Serious Problem?

Chapter Preface

The face of homelessness has changed over the years. In the past, most Americans envisioned the homeless as mentally ill or substance-abusing vagrants who lived on the streets of large cities. As the supply of affordable housing began to shrink in the 1980s, however, the need for emergency shelter grew, as did national awareness of the growing problem of homelessness among American families. According to the National Coalition for the Homeless, the fastest growing segment of the homeless population are families with children. Indeed, the 2005 U.S. Conference of Mayors survey of hunger and homelessness revealed that 33 percent of the nation's homeless population are families with children. Unfortunately, the survey reports, of those families requesting shelter, 32 percent were denied shelter due to a lack of resources. One of several controversies in the homelessness debate is, therefore, the impact of the growing number of homeless families.

One of the primary concerns expressed by homeless advocates is the impact of homelessness on the health of children in homeless families. According to the National Center on Family Homelessness, "homeless children get sick twice as often as other children." The center reports that homeless children have twice as many ear infections, four times as many asthma attacks, five times more stomach problems, six times as many speech problems, and twice as many hospitalizations. Due to the trauma of homelessness, many homeless children also have more mental health problems than do children who are not homeless. "More than 20% of homeless preschoolers have emotional problems serious enough to require professional care. 47% of homeless school-age children have problems such as anxiety, depression, or withdrawal, compared to 18% of other children," the center maintains.

Due in part to these physical and mental health problems, many homeless children also have problems in school. The fact that some schools do not allow homeless children to register without records or a home address further aggravates the problem. In some cases, transportation to school is not available to shelter children. As a result, the National Center on Family Homelessness reports, homeless children are four times more likely to have developmental delays, twice as likely to have learning disabilities, and twice as likely to repeat a grade, often due to frequent absence or moves to new schools.

While homelessness appears to have many negative effects on children, some advocates claim that homeless families have positive characteristics that with the implementation of appropriate policies could improve the chances of America's homeless children. According to childhood education professor Kevin J. Swick, the heads of homeless families have fewer substance abuse and mental health problems than individuals who are homeless. Moreover, they are more likely to be employed and less likely to engage in antisocial behavior. Homeless families also tend to be homeless for shorter periods, and the parents are more actively engaged in ways to empower themselves. "Success stories of homeless women and their children attaining more self-sufficiency indicates that paying attention early on to homelessness in young families is crucial," Swick asserts. In his view, the particular situation that a homeless family faces should determine the type of services they need. While a middle-class homeless mother seeking shelter from an abusive spouse may need a combination of short-term services and counseling, "more intensive services are likely to be needed for the chronically poor and persistently homeless family," he maintains.

Analysts continue to examine the nature and scope of family homelessness to develop policies that will best help America's homeless children. The authors in the following chapter explore the seriousness of other issues in the homelessness controversy.

> "The number of people experiencing hunger and homelessness is rising, and communities are strained for resources to deal with these issues."

Homelessness Is a Widespread Problem

National Student Campaign Against Hunger & Homelessness

Homelessness and hunger are growing problems nationwide, claims the National Student Campaign Against Hunger & Homelessness (NSCAHH) in the following viewpoint. The problem is not limited to urban areas, the student action group maintains, but is also increasing in small towns and rural areas. Since the 1980s, churches and charitable organizations have recognized the need for food banks and shelters to feed and house the growing homeless population, NSCAHH asserts, yet government funds to address the problem are decreasing, making it difficult for American communities to cope.

As you read, consider the following questions:

1. In the opinion of NSCAHH, what cue should Americans have taken from the 1930s, 1940s, and 1980s?

National Student Campaign Against Hunger & Homelessness, "Hunger and Homelessness in Our Communities," *Communities in Crisis: A Survey of Hunger & Homelessness in America 2004*, February 2005, pp. 5–9. Reproduced by permission.

2. According to the author, from what two programs that respond to homelessness has the government cut funding?

3. What was the average reported increase in the number of shelter requests from 2003 to 2004, based on the author's 2004 survey?

"I don't understand why we have so much poverty in the richest country in the world!"—Alfredzine Black, YWCA of Marion, Indiana

E ven though the United States is the richest country in the world, millions of Americans experience hunger and homelessness each year. Approximately 3.5 million people are homeless each year, while 36.3 million live in households without enough food.

A Growing Problem

Official reports of poverty and hunger show that the number of people at risk of hunger and homelessness is growing. From 2002 to 2003, the number of people living in poverty in the United States increased by 1.3 million to 35.9 million. Predictably, rates of hunger are rising along with poverty. In 2003, the number of people living in food-insecure households rose for the third year in a row to 36.3 million Americans, including more than 13 million children.

Over the past 25 years, a vast network of emergency food and shelter providers has sprung up to deal with growing hunger and homelessness in America. Food pantries, kitchens, and shelters existed before 1980 but were not common. A deep recession and severe cuts to social programs in the early 1980s led to a visible increase in the number of homeless and hungry Americans. As a result, more people turned to churches and charitable agencies for help, and those agencies grew in number and size. In 1980, there were about two dozen food banks nationwide; today, there are more than 200 affiliated

Percent of Agencies in Sample Urban or Small to Mid-Sized Towns & Rural Areas Reporting an Increase in Shelter Requests			
Urban		**Small/Mid-sized Towns**	
Miami	100%	Massachusetts	100%
Washington, DC	86%	Pennsylvania	70%
Pittsburgh	78%	Connecticut	60%
Los Angeles	70%	Wisconsin	50%

with America's Second Harvest, the food bank network, and several dozen additional independent food banks. Food pantries and kitchens are now a common site in communities; Bread for the World Institute estimates 150,000 food programs nationwide. The number of shelters also has skyrocketed. A study by the Urban Institute found that the number of shelter beds available in the U.S. rose from 275,000 in 1988 to more than 607,000 used on an average night in 1996.

The Risks of Cutting Funding

Although the number of people experiencing hunger and homelessness continues to grow, government funds to address these problems are down. Elected officials would do well to take a cue from history. We learned in the 1930s and 1940s that enacting a comprehensive safety net, including affordable housing and nutritious food assistance, can successfully help bring millions out of poverty; conversely, we learned in the 1980s that severe cuts to social programs will increase hunger and homelessness.

Despite these lessons, the U.S. government and states are reducing funding to critical programs. In 2002 and 2003, nearly every state experienced a fiscal crisis; many dealt with these crises by cutting budget allocations for social programs, including grants to homeless shelters and feeding programs. Federal funding for social programs, already inadequate, has been on the chopping block recently. Funding for the primary federal response to homelessness, the McKinney Vento Homeless Assistance Programs, has been insufficient since its inception and, in 2004, was cut $19 million by Congress. Funding for the premier affordable housing program, the "Section 8" Housing Choice Voucher Program, is only sufficient to help one in four eligible households, yet the [George W.] Bush Administration and Congress continue to propose billion-dollar cuts.

Responses ... from 900 emergency food and shelter providers indicate that government cuts to social programs are out of step with reality. The number of people experiencing hunger and homelessness is rising, and communities are strained for resources to deal with these issues. This is true in every state surveyed, spanning a variety of large cities, small towns, and rural areas. Despite strong community responses, the increase in hunger and homelessness combined with funding cuts is leaving many communities in crisis. . . .

Increasing Emergency Shelter Requests

The 2004 Survey of Hunger and Homelessness in America [coordinated by the National Student Campaign Against Hunger & Homelessness] found that 66% of emergency shelters surveyed reported an increase in the number of shelter requests [in 2004] as compared to [2003]. The average reported increase was 27%. Further, 50% of agencies surveyed reported an increase in the length of stay for shelter clients compared [to 2003] and 57% reported an increase as compared [to 2000].

As with food requests, this increase is a national trend. Agencies in every state surveyed except Kansas reported an increase in requests for emergency shelter. Massachusetts, Iowa, and Virginia had the highest percentages of agencies reporting an increase in requests for emergency shelter assistance, 93%, 89%, and 81%, respectively. Agencies in New Jersey, Pennsylvania, North Carolina, and Texas reported the highest percentage increases in requests for shelter assistance, 75%, 35%, 32%, and 32%, respectively.

As with food, increases in shelter requests were reported by agencies in every type of community, including large cities, small towns, and rural areas. . . . A high percentage of agencies reported increasing need from urban Los Angeles and Miami to rural areas in Massachusetts and Pennsylvania.

These findings are indicative of an increase in homelessness nationwide. Corroborating data is sparse, as the government does no large-scale study of homelessness as it does of hunger, but the aforementioned increase in poverty—from 31.1 million to 35.9 million from 2000 to 2003—does indicate the potential for an increase in homelessness. In addition, the U.S. Conference of Mayors 2004 survey found that 70% of the 27 urban areas surveyed saw an increase in requests for emergency shelter [in 2004].

A Diverse Impact

Responses from the 900 agencies surveyed indicate a significant increase in the number of people experiencing hunger and homelessness across the country. This is a problem in a diverse range of communities, from towns of 1000 people like Turtle Lake, Wisconsin, to suburbs like McKeesport, Pennsylvania, to major cities like Los Angeles, California.

Increasing hunger and homelessness is not a new phenomenon in our communities. In response, citizens, business, and governments have a long history of contributing money, goods, and time to help meet the need of low-income Americans, generosity that has alleviated hunger and homelessness for millions.

Unfortunately, . . . the combination of decreasing resources in these times of rising need is overwhelming ability of communities to help those in need and leaving many low income individuals with nowhere to turn.

> *"It serves the interests of activists to broaden the definition [of homelessness] and exaggerate the numbers in order to gain public sympathy and taxpayer dollars."*

The Problem of Homelessness Is Exaggerated

Mike Rosen

To gain public sympathy and taxpayer dollars, activists exaggerate homeless estimates, argues Denver, Colorado, radio talk-show host Mike Rosen in the following viewpoint. Broad definitions that include people temporarily living with friends and relatives inflate homeless counts, he claims. Moreover, Rosen maintains, the homeless often use multiple services and are sometimes counted twice. Because homelessness is caused by multiple factors requiring unique solutions, Rosen reasons, using these flawed strategies to obtain inflated homeless counts distorts the problem and leads to simplistic solutions.

As you read, consider the following questions:

1. According to Rosen, to what did activist Mitch Snyder confess after estimating America's homeless at 3 million?

2. How were the homeless defined in Denver's homeless survey, according to the author?

3. In Rosen's opinion, how many people in Denver were identified as "chronically homeless"?

Ten thousand homeless in Denver! That's the claim of an activist group, The Metropolitan Denver Homeless Initiative. The coalition wants more money and programs to address the problem in the seven-county metro area.

Pulling Figures out of Thin Air

Ever since Mitch Snyder pulled the figure of "3 million homeless" out of thin air, the art of estimating the homeless population has become a political football. The highly theatrical Snyder, you may recall, was the founder of something called the "Community for Creative Non-Violence." Apparently, fabricating self-serving statistics is a form of such creativity.

Snyder first testified, before a congressional committee in 1981, that 1.2 million Americans were homeless. By 1983, he had elevated the figure to 3 million. The media, generally sympathetic to his cause, embraced Snyder's number and spread it far and wide. In 1984, the Department of Housing and Urban Development attempted a more scientific study and came up with its own estimate of 250,000–350,000, and the Census Bureau, a few months later, arrived at 240,000.

Snyder later confessed that he was just satisfying the media's lust for a figure, so he made some perfunctory phone calls to homeless providers then issued his exaggerated numbers. As he told Ted Koppel on *Nightline*, "They have no meaning, no value." (Synder also proclaimed to a college audience that 45 homeless people die every second in this country. If you do the math, that comes to 23 million deaths a year exceeding many times over his own inflated estimate of the total homeless population.)

I don't how many homeless there are, and neither does anyone else.

The Importance of Accurate Numbers

Getting an accurate estimate of the number of homeless, matters. If we believe the number is huge, the cry of "crisis" will resound through the land, and government will throw more money. . . . If we believe the number is small, we can remain calm enough to analyze the problem and look for efficient policies.

The number of homeless most commonly cited in the media is 3,000,000, a number scary enough to trigger an uproar. Is this figure the result of a scientific study? Not at all. It is an arbitrary number thrown to the media.

Gerald and Natalie Sinkin,
New Fairfield (CT) Citizen News, *January 4, 1989.*

A Confusing Definition

Compounding the confusion is the very definition of what constitutes "homelessness." Since it serves the interests of activists to broaden the definition and exaggerate the numbers in order to gain public sympathy and taxpayer dollars for their cause, it's useful to cut through the hype.

Are there really 10,000 homeless people in Denver? I've studied the survey. Tom Leuhrs, the chair of the Denver group that commissioned it, was cooperative, but his answers to my questions didn't inspire confidence in its accuracy. As with other surveys of this type, seeking to capture an elusive population that accesses multiple services, it's vulnerable to double counting.

All information is extrapolated from one day's headcount—Jan. 27, 2003—during the coldest part of winter when shelters tend to overflow. The definition of homeless includes anyone "without an independent, permanent address." That means your 22-year-old daughter, out of college and temporarily between jobs, may be regarded as homeless if she moves back in with mom and dad.

If your mental image of the homeless is one of people sleeping under a bridge or in a doorway, you'll find this study includes far more comfortable venues.

Twenty-eight percent are already accommodated in transitional housing, 28 percent are living with a friend or relative (this is construed as "doubling up," and regarded as a form of homelessness), 10 percent are in a hotel or motel. That accounts for two-thirds of the "homeless," including almost all of the children in families. Nineteen percent are in emergency shelters. Another 5 percent are in medical or psychiatric hospitals, detox facilities, jails, domestic violence shelters, migrant shelters or, curiously, "In a home I/We own." Only 10 percent are on the streets, under bridges, in cars, buses or camping out.

In a recent *Denver Post* editorial, I learned that under the stricter definition of "chronically homeless"—those who have been homeless for more than a year, or have been homeless at least four times in the past three years, or have disabilities—only 540 people, not 10,000, in Denver are so identified.

Homelessness is a product of many different causes, affecting dramatically different people, calling for vastly different public policy responses. Subsidized housing, child care and a job may be the answer for an abandoned mother with young children. Effective remedies for prematurely emancipated mental patients, drunks, drug addicts, hobos, and runaway kids are more elusive. Whatever value there may be in this Denver survey is not to be found in sensationalistic claims simplifying and distorting the problem.

"Rural homelessness has always taken a back seat to the more glaring problems in cities."

Rural Homelessness Is a Serious Problem

Randal C. Archibold

In the following viewpoint Randal C. Archibold claims that the problem of rural homelessness is often obscured by the more conspicuous homeless problem in urban areas. Although not as glaring, he maintains, many rural residents have been left homeless due to local economic problems and rising housing costs. Without help from federal agencies, Archibold argues, rural communities are finding it difficult to cope. Despite great need, Archibold asserts, rural communities often do not receive needed funding because required head counts are difficult to obtain in rural areas. Archibold is a staff writer for the New York Times.

As you read, consider the following questions:

1. What percentage of the homeless nationwide are from small towns, according to studies cited by Archibold?
2. What does shelter director Lance Cheslock, as cited by the author, mean by "Greyhound therapy"?

3. Why does the National Coalition on Homelessness think the Agriculture Department should handle rural homelessness, according to Archibold?

As the [George W.] Bush administration promotes a widely praised multibillion-dollar effort to end chronic homelessness in cities like Washington and San Francisco, a growing outcry is rising from rural areas that worsening problems far away from urban centers are being overlooked.

Taking a Back Seat

Rural homelessness has always taken a back seat to the more glaring problems in cities. Most studies estimate homeless people in small towns account for about 9 percent of the 600,000 or so homeless nationwide. But local officials and advocates for the homeless in small towns say that economic distress in recent years, including closing plants, failing farms, rising housing costs and other troubles, has left more people without homes and in greater need of help.

Real numbers are hard to come by because most rural areas, where homeless services often means ad hoc help from church groups or volunteers, are far behind a parade of cities taking head counts.

"We are concerned that the focus on chronic homelessness may have the unintended consequence of shifting services away from families and rural communities," said John Parvensky, executive director of the Colorado Coalition for the Homeless, one of several groups pushing the federal government to turn more attention to rural areas.

Among the homeless [in rural Trinidad, Colorado,] is John Lobato, who offered a tour of his surroundings—the abandoned shuttle bus where he sometimes sleeps, the makeshift assortment of pallets, mattresses and blankets where he and other men pass time, often drinking, and the Purgatoire River, where he bathes.

Sometimes he takes his medicine for schizophrenia, Mr. Lobato said, sometimes not. Sometimes he sobers up for a while, but then the bottle calls.

"I know I need help," he said, before embarking on a search for a liquor fix at midday in this isolated town 180 miles south of Denver. "But I don't know where to get it."

Greyhound Therapy

Until recently, many small towns like Trinidad coped with those who panhandled or set up makeshift encampments in the woods with what Lance Cheslock, director of La Puente, a shelter in Alamosa, near [Trinidad], calls "Greyhound therapy." They handed out bus tickets.

"They just send them up to the cities and let them deal with the problem there," said Mr. Cheslock, among the advocates pushing for a new way to finance rural homeless programs.

The growing visibility of the problem has made some towns reconsider that attitude and push for local solutions, although they can be expensive and difficult.

Rural homelessness "doesn't get enough attention," said Philip Mangano, the executive director of the United States Interagency Council on Homelessness and the Bush administration's chief coordinator of homeless services. But Mr. Mangano said the problem had been difficult to assess because rural communities by and large had not chronicled their problems with the data-heavy planning documents the Housing and Urban Development Department and other federal agencies demand.

"Like any profile of the homeless, there is a lot of anecdote and hearsay, but you need data and research to create policy," Mr. Mangano said.

To confront the problem, he cited the examples of Washington and Michigan, where every county, many of them rural, has committed to writing a plan to end homelessness.

A Serious Problem in Rural America

Homelessness is a serious and growing problem in rural areas throughout the United States. While homeless persons are less numerous in rural than in urban areas, the proportionate incidences of homelessness in some rural counties are similar to or greater than those found in major metropolitan areas. For rural communities with few health and social services, the burden of homelessness is disproportionately heavy.

Patricia A. Post, National Health Care for the Homeless Council,
January 2002.

A Community Looks for Solutions

Here in Trinidad, a former old West coal town of 9,000 near the eastern slopes of the Sangre de Cristo mountains, people have long struggled through hard times. The downtown is pockmarked with shuttered storefronts, but new cafes and galleries have opened as the town tries to refashion itself as an artists' colony.

Interstate 25, dotted with motels of various quality and shopping centers, slices through Trinidad, leaving tidy Victorian homes rising on a hill on one side and modest ranches, several in disrepair, on the other.

Sandi Espinoza, who directs the Open Door Soup Kitchen, in space borrowed from a church, said the organization was serving more meals than ever—families, veterans, men just released from prison and a wide assortment of people smelling of liqour before noon. Some 85 people come daily for lunch, double the number from a few years ago, Ms. Espinoza said. "We need shelter here," said one wobbly man, who when asked where he sleeps, replied, "down under the bridges."

There is no homeless shelter, only a few drug, alcohol or mental illness treatment programs for the indigent, and a loose group of church pastors, volunteers and other concerned citizens striving to look after people who have no home.

"Pastor helps me out," Mr. Lobato said. "The soup kitchen helps me out and these guys"—he motioned to his disheveled companions—"help me, too."

A couple of weeks ago, officials here cheered the establishment of a "transitional housing unit," a single-family home leased from the government for $1 a year where a displaced family can live for a year or so until they get back on their feet, the first such project started here. The organizers say several families, doubled up with relatives or friends, need a place like that.

There is nothing for the men living in the tents and shacks that have popped up behind the Wal-Mart.

To seek more stable solutions, a small group was recently formed. With guidance from Becky Vanderslice, an organizer with Housing Justice, a group based in Denver, they gathered around a church conference table and discussed problems that included the need for rehabilitation programs and families unable to make ends meet.

Finally, said Cary T. Nelson, pastor at First Christian Church, the group decided to start with the single-family home. Churches and volunteers will subsidize the costs of running the house, a foreclosed property held by the local office of the federal Agriculture Department.

They called the house Haven of Hope and have begun searching for a family to occupy it. One applicant, Brenda Holguin, said she hoped to move in with at least two of her four children, who are living with her estranged husband. A domestic dispute has left her homeless, living in a nearby domestic violence shelter, and such a house would help set her on a steady path, Ms. Holguin said. "Having a house, my family in one place, would give me more self-esteem," she said.

Ms. Espinoza, who runs the soup kitchen, said she was hoping that local businesses or churches would step forward with donated space for an emergency shelter.

Getting Help for Rural Areas

The National Coalition on Homelessness, an advocacy group, is considering mounting an effort to make the Agriculture Department, with its many field offices and staff members in rural areas, the lead agency for financing homeless programs outside urban areas. The task currently falls to the Department of Housing and Urban Development [HUD].

"It should be the department of housing and urban-only development," said Michael Stoops, the executive director of the coalition. "We should not give up on HUD, but we need to get other federal agencies involved." [In 2005], he said, HUD provided $120 million for 700 projects in rural areas, an amount that federal officials say has remained constant for several years. [In 2006], the federal government has increased direct spending on homeless programs to about $4 billion, up from $2.9 billion and double the spending of [2001]. About 10 percent of that has gone toward a new focus on ending chronic homelessness, Mr. Mangano said.

The approach has fired up hope in Denver, San Francisco, Washington and other cities that headway is being made, but it has dismayed advocates in rural areas, where grant-writing expertise and the Talmudic knowledge of federal regulations are lacking.

Small towns also lack the network of nonprofit organizations and corporations that often underwrite efforts.

"The government wants matching funds and the big city funders only fund the big cities," said Donna Haddow, a member of the Trinidad-Las Animas County Economic Development Board. "There's nothing left by the time we come knocking."

Ms. Vanderslice of Housing Justice said a prominent foundation would not finance the new housing program in Trinidad because it had decided to focus most of its resources on Denver.

"There is a lot of money to end homelessness in the state," she said. "But a lot is going to the Denver metro area because the mayor there has a 10-year plan."

Here, she added, "they are going on open faith."

> "One of every three homeless adult males sleeping in a doorway, alley, box, car, [or] barn ... has served our nation in the Armed Forces."

Homelessness Is a Serious Problem for Many U.S. Military Veterans

National Coalition for Homeless Veterans

More than five hundred thousand U.S. veterans experience homelessness each year, maintains the National Coalition for Homeless Veterans (NCHV) in the following viewpoint. Fractured family relationships, addiction, and post-traumatic stress disorder—all a direct result of military service—contribute to a high risk of homelessness among veterans. Contrary to public opinion, the coalition claims, many veterans do not receive the support they need. In fact, the NCHV asserts, the income of more than 1.5 million veterans falls below the poverty line. The NCHV provides housing for homeless veterans nationwide.

As you read, consider the following questions:

1. According to the NCHV, during what military conflicts have homeless veterans served?

National Coalition for Homeless Veterans, "Statement for Record, House Veterans Subcommittee on Oversight and Investigations," May 19, 2005. www.nchv.org. Reproduced by permission.

2. In the author's opinion, what percentage of homeless veterans are served annually by the VA?

3. What program does the NCHV believe provides the best opportunity to alert servicemembers to the risk of homelessness?

The VA [Veterans Administration] estimates that approximately 250,000 veterans are homeless on any given night; more than 500,000 experience homelessness over the course of a year. Conservatively, one of every three homeless adult males sleeping in a doorway, alley, box, car, barn or other location not fit for human habitation in our urban, suburban, and rural communities has served our nation in the Armed Forces. Homeless veterans are mostly males (2 percent are females). 54 percent are people of color. The vast majority are single, although service providers are reporting an increased number of veterans with children seeking their assistance. 45 percent have mental illness. 50 percent have an addiction.

Who Are Homeless Veterans?

America's homeless veterans have served in World War II, Korea, the Cold War, Vietnam, Grenada, Panama, Lebanon, anti-drug cultivation efforts in South America, Afghanistan, and Iraq. 47 percent of homeless veterans served during the Vietnam Era. More than 67 percent served our nation for at least three years and 33 percent were stationed in a war zone.

Male veterans are twice as likely to become homeless as their non-veteran counterparts, and female veterans are about four times as likely to become homeless as their non-veteran counterparts. Like their non-veteran counterparts, veterans are at high risk of homelessness due to extremely low or no income, dismal living conditions in cheap hotels or in overcrowded or substandard housing, and lack of access to health care. In addition to these shared factors, a large number of at-risk veterans live with post traumatic stress disorders [PTSDs] and addictions acquired during or exacerbated by their military service. In addition, their family and social networks are fractured due to lengthy periods away from their communities of origin. These problems are directly traceable to their experience in military service or to their return to civilian society without appropriate transitional supports.

Veterans Are Not All Well Supported

Contrary to the perceptions that our nation's veterans are well supported, in fact many go without the services they require and are eligible to receive. One and a half million veterans have incomes that fan below the federal poverty level. Neither the VA, state or county departments of veteran affairs, nor community-based and faith-based service providers are adequately resourced to respond to these veterans' health, housing, and supportive services needs. For example, the VA reports that its homeless treatment and community-based assistance network serves 100,000 veterans annually. With an estimated 500,000 veterans experiencing homelessness at some time during a year and the VA reaching only 20 percent of those in need, 400,000 veterans remain without services from the department responsible for supporting them. Likewise, other federal, state, and local public agencies—notably housing and health departments—are not adequately responding to the housing, health care and supportive services needs of veterans. Indeed, it appears that veterans fail to register as a target group for these agencies. . . .

The Problem of Injured Servicemembers

NCHV shares the [House] Committee's interest in ensuring that those of our nation's servicemembers who have sustained severe or debilitating injuries in the line of duty are provided the transition assistance necessary for physical stabilization, emotional recovery, physical and mental rehabilitation, and es-

Homelessness a Rising Problem Among Iraq Vets

Veterans of the Iraq and Afghanistan conflicts are now showing up in the nation's homeless shelters.

While the numbers are still small, they're steadily rising, and raising alarms in both the homeless and veterans communities. The concern is that these returning veterans— some of whom can't find jobs after leaving the military, others of whom are still struggling psychologically with the war—may be just the beginning of an influx of new veterans in need. Currently, there are 150,000 troops in Iraq and 16,000 in Afghanistan. More than 130,000 have already served and returned home.

Alexandra Marks, Christian Science Monitor, *February 8, 2005.*

tablishment of independent living, or fully-supported living when complete independence is no longer possible.

Like our fellow Americans, we have watched our servicemembers, through weekly news coverage, in awe and gratitude as one after the other amazing story of survival, courage, and hope is reported to us. We have watched as some of our seriously injured servicemembers heal their wounds, re-learn basic skills, and leave DOD [Department of Defense] or VA medical facilities on their own means or with extensive family supports in place. We are also heartened in the knowledge that the Department of Defense, Department of Veterans Affairs and other federal, state, local, and private agencies and their dedicated professionals have organized their resources and talents—some more successfully than others—to support these servicemembers in their return to civilian life.

Yet, we know that for each such successful transition, there is an equal or greater share of heartache—injured servicemembers for whom the return from battle is anything but seamless. These are the servicemembers whose injuries, while serious, are not so grossly severe that military commanders have flagged them for priority attention. These are the servicemembers whose family members—if they even have strong family supports—are unsure how "the system" works and how to become patient advocates or public relations operatives. These are the servicemembers being caught between multiple federal, state, and county military and veterans agencies still struggling to share information with each other. And naturally, these are the servicemembers so poorly supported by our presumed "Grade A" military personnel and veterans affairs' systems that they become homeless.

A Tragic Story

Take Venessa Turner. Ms. Turner joined the U.S. Army in April 1997 and advanced to the rank of sergeant. She was deployed to Camp Balad, 20 miles west of Baghdad, in Operation Iraqi Freedom. While serving in the combat theater, she collapsed in 130-degree heat, fell into a coma, and nearly died of heart failure. She was evacuated to Europe, then to Walter Reed Army Medical Center in Washington, D.C., and released with a pending medical discharge in July 2003. And that is the good part of Ms. Turner's story.

Ms. Turner was released from Walter Reed—and discharged from the military—with neither a place to live nor ongoing health care in place. Without a home, she and her daughter bounced from place to place—from the couch in her mother's cramped one-bedroom apartment, to a friend's couch, to her sister's friend's friend's couch. When she went to the Veterans Affairs Medical Center in West Roxbury, [Massachussetts,] she was told she had to wait three months to see a doctor. When she asked the Army to ship her possessions from her unit's base in Germany, where she had lived with her daughter for more than a year, they told her she had to fly back at her own expense to get them herself. And when she sought help to secure a veterans' loan for a house in Boston, she said mortgage brokers told her the only real option was to move to Springfield or Worcester. Ms. Turner's tragic situation was partially resolved only with the persistent intervention of a Member of Congress.

Regrettably, there are dozens more Vanessa Turners returning from Iraq and Afghanistan without a place to call home. Not all of them know to call their Member of Congress for relief—nor should they have to! The community-based homeless veteran service providers that NCHV represents are reporting servicemembers from Operation Enduring Freedom and Operation Iraqi Freedom among their service users. Some of these newly homeless veterans are seriously injured. Others are fighting PTSD and other emotional and addictive impairments. Still others simply have been unable to find work. Regardless of the cause, in a country as wealthy as the United States, with the best military personnel and veteran support systems in the world, it is simply outrageous that any servicemember or former servicemember becomes homeless.

NCHV is generally supportive of the various federal government-wide, joint service, and service-specific initiatives underway to assist severely injured servicemembers in transitioning to civilian life. . . . These service coordination and transition assistance initiatives are a vast improvement over the poor treatment that servicemembers in previous campaigns received upon their return home. These focused initiatives provide opportunities for servicemembers, family members, public officials, and veterans' service organizations to detect multiservice needs and plug system gaps. . . .

The Importance of Outreach

Servicemembers separating from the Armed Forces, including servicemembers separating due to serious injuries, receive opportunities to learn about benefits for which they may be eligible, both prior to separation (through preseparation counseling and the Transition Assistance Program) and postdischarge via Department of Veterans Affairs outreach. VA outreach provides an opportunity, as yet untapped, to alert recently separated servicemembers to the increased risk of homelessness they face and the preventative service available to them if they find themselves at imminent risk of losing their living arrangement. . . .

Individuals leaving the military are at high risk of homelessness due to a lack of job skills transferable to the civilian sector, disrupted or dissolved family and social support networks, and other risk factors that preceded their military service. Separating servicemembers must be made aware of the factors that contribute to homelessness and receive information about sources of preventive assistance before they exit the military.

A robust outreach program not only informs veterans of services available to them should they become homeless, but also to guide them on steps they may take to avert homelessness. Congress should require VA outreach plans and outreach efforts to add homelessness prevention matter as expected outreach content, including information on risk factors for homelessness, a self-assessment of risk factors, and contact information for preventative assistance associated with homelessness.

Current law (38 U.S.C. 2022) requires VA, in its outreach program, to target veterans being discharged or released from institutions after inpatient care. Congress should add as an additional target population individuals separating from the armed forces.

The National Coalition for Homeless Veterans looks forward to continuing to work with the Committee on Veterans' Affairs in ensuring that our nation does everything within its grasp to ensure a seamless transition for our nation's separating servicemembers. These soldiers have served our nation well. It is beyond time for us to repay the debt.

"The next big wave of homeless people in America will be foster kids."

Homelessness Is a Serious Problem Among Foster Children

Kevin Fagan

Newly emancipated foster children born during the crack cocaine epidemic of the 1980s are the next wave of America's homeless, maintains San Francisco Chronicle *reporter Kevin Fagan in the following viewpoint. Many foster children do not have the education or life skills needed to maintain a home, he asserts. Before they enter the system, Fagan claims, foster children often experience physical abuse at the hands of drug addicted and/or mentally ill parents, and some remain troubled or are themselves addicted to drugs, factors that increase the risk of homelessness.*

As you read, consider the following questions:

1. What percentage of emancipated foster youth face homelessness in California, according to the California Department of Social Services, as cited by the author?

2. According to Fagan, by what percentage did the number of foster children increase nationally between 1982 and 1990?

3. In what four cities does the author claim that the number of foster youth who are "aging out" is expected to grow?

Darnell Bailey sat on the stoop of his cramped apartment building at the edge of San Francisco's Chinatown, head in his hands. He wiped a tear off one cheek, stared hard at the traffic and stood up.

Bailey had just come back that morning from the East Bay, where he and one of his six brothers rescued his 17-year-old half-sister from her own mother, who was pimping her on the street in Richmond [California]. A few days before that, he had been fired at an upscale restaurant for being late—because he was washing his uniform at a Laundromat after coming home, late, from back-to-back shifts.

Helping Foster Kids in Danger

A couple years ago, trouble like this all at once could have spelled disaster for this 20-year-old former foster kid with a juvenile record for drugs and theft. That's back when he was homeless—like thousands of other youths in the United States each year who emerge from the troubled foster care system with so little hope that they wind up on the street.

But Bailey has an ace in the hole. It's the reason why, when he started walking on this particular day of bad news, he wasn't looking for the nearest drug dealer. He headed uptown to a counselor.

Bailey is one of 31 former foster children enrolled in the Larkin Extended Aftercare for Supported Emancipation Program (LEASE), the city's first-ever full-service program specifically targeting foster kids in danger of becoming homeless as they move out on their own at age 18. It gives them something most of them have never had: an apartment of their own, with steady counseling for everything from substance abuse to job hunting.

The three-year pilot program, which hopes to serve 80 kids overall, comes at a crucial time.

The Next Wave of Homeless Americans

The next big wave of homeless people in America will be foster kids, experts say, and from New York to the Bay Area, cities and counties are trying to get ready for it. One of the main reasons: The children of crack addicts, born when the crack epidemic exploded in the mid-1980s, have matured to young adults and are starting to show up in the gutter, angry, homeless and addicted themselves.

The California Department of Social Services estimates 65 percent of emancipated foster youth in the state face homelessness as soon as they are turned loose from the system—and up to 50 percent actually wind up sleeping in the street. That's a lot of kids, considering there are now 90,000 foster children in the state and 4,000 of them "age out" of the system every year.

Prospects are just as dim for the remaining 630,000 foster kids throughout the United States, said Celeste Bodner, executive director of Foster Club, a national support group based in Oregon.

Observers say LEASE, which opened its doors in December [2003] under contract with the city Department of Human Services, is the most promising of all the methods being undertaken to address the crisis.

Now, instead of turning to the methamphetamine he might have turned to years ago to ease his despair over his sister, or over losing his job, Bailey can turn to Larkin's social workers for comfort—which is what he did. And instead of hitting the sidewalk with a sleeping bag because he can't afford a place to

The Relationship Between Foster Care and Homelessness

- There is an over-representation of people with a foster care history in the homeless population.

- Homeless people with a foster care history are more likely than other people to have their own children in foster care.

- Very frequently, people who are homeless had multiple placements as children: some were in foster care, but others were "unofficial" placements in the homes of family or friends.

- Those people with a foster care history tend to become homeless at an earlier age than those who do not have a foster care history.

- Homeless people who are white are somewhat more likely to have a foster care history than people who are Hispanic or African American.

- Childhood placement in foster care can correlate with a substantial increase in the length of a person's homeless experience.

Nan P. Roman and Phyllis Wolfe,
National Alliance to End Homelessness, April 1995.

stay, Bailey knows Larkin will cover his rent and help him find other work—which is what it did.

"I might be either on dope or dead if not for these guys," Bailey said, heading off to catch a bus to Larkin to interview for a job helping supervise the agency's day-laborer program (which he got a week later). "I know my life is up to me, but sometimes you just need a little help.

"Now I have that help. People want me to succeed. I'm going to make it."

A Hand Up, Not a Handout

The thrust of Larkin's program is in keeping with what the nationally lauded agency has been doing for 20 years for homeless youths and runaways in San Francisco, LEASE director Sam Cobbs said. It gives a hand up, not a handout.

"Some programs provide education for kids. Others might help them with a bed," Cobbs said. "But we give it all, and at a crucial time of these young people's lives, where they will either slip off the track or build lives for themselves. We help them build those lives."

Bailey and the other youths in the program are assigned case managers who hook them up with as many as a dozen services teaching them everything from how to fill out a resume and get into college to how to master "life skills," such as washing laundry or scrambling eggs. The programs also offer emotional counseling, drug abuse counseling and medical care, as well as close interaction with other programs in the city such as the Independent Living Skills Program, which gives job, house-hunting and other training to emancipated foster kids.

The youths are housed in apartments all over the city, and they pay 30 percent of their income in rent, no matter what that income is, with LEASE picking up the rest. They can stay until they are 21 years old, but even after that, the intention is to keep in touch with counselors to make sure everything goes OK post-program.

This is exactly the type of "supportive housing" program a special committee headed by former [San Francisco City] Supervisor Angela Alioto intends to call for as it assembles a 10-year plan to end chronic homelessness in San Francisco. "Preventing someone from becoming chronically homeless is every bit as important as helping them get off the street," Alioto said—and that's what the new program is all about.

"A lot of foster kids never had a place of their own, never got to cook their own meals," said Rebecca Cherin, who as director of Larkin's employment training also helps manage LEASE. "There's this assumption that when you get out of high school, you're going to college, getting your own place and starting an exciting new life.

"But not if you're a foster kid. You too often get a handshake and the door."

A Flood of Foster Children

Since the early 1990s nationwide, about 20,000 foster kids have turned 18 every year, but that will at least double in the next several years as the flood of children who entered the system during the mid-1980s crack epidemic become adults.

"Everyone is just now starting to brace for it," said Bodner, the chief of the Foster Club support group.

But apparently that won't be enough.

"Larkin's program is very exciting, but programs like it are very few and far between," said Jill Duerr-Berrick, a social welfare professor at UC Berkeley who is one of the nation's leading experts on foster care. "We need a whole lot more resources poured into the situation."

Nationally, the number of foster children increased 64 percent between 1982 and 1990, at the height of the crack epidemic, she said—a stunning rise considering the number of children born overall in the country only grew 1 percent during the same period.

Those foster children from the 1980s are turning 18 now. San Francisco—one of the nation's four centers for growth in foster youth populations "aging out," along with Los Angeles, New York and Chicago—expects about 850 kids to move out on their own over the next five years [2004–2009], said Maggie Donahue of the city Department of Human Services. That's a big jump from the 663 who aged out of the system over the previous five years.

"It's the next big wave, and we want to make sure they don't all just wind up in homeless shelters or on the street,"

Donahue said. "We have other good programs that help homeless kids, but (LEASE) is different. It's about preventing the kids becoming homeless to begin with."

An Investment in the Future

Larkin's program costs $837,000 a year to run, and $334,800 of that comes from the state under its new Transitional Housing Plus Supportive Services program, which is earmarked specifically for fosters becoming emancipated. Seven other counties, including Contra Costa and Alameda [in the Bay Area], will be using the state funds to start versions of Larkin's program in the coming year—and Alameda already has started an alternative that concentrates on teenagers who are pregnant or are mothers.

The total tab, statewide, is expected to be $6 million annually over the next three years. The funding is proposed for cuts in the state budget battle, which Donahue said should set off alarm bells for any planners looking to save money in the long run.

She pointed out that it costs $16,800 a year to serve and house a kid in LEASE—compared to $23,000 to put that same kid in a shelter, $60,000 to put him in jail or $54,000 to put him in a hospital.

"What better investment can you make for the future?" Donahue asked.

Waiting for Success

When Bailey moved into his studio apartment on Bush Street, it was the first time he'd lived on his own. A few doors down the hall is 18-year-old Ulili Ononvakpuri, who is also now living on her own for the first time under the LEASE program.

While just a few months ago they had little idea what the future held, the typical afternoon now finds Bailey and Ononvakpuri refining their resumes at Larkin's Sutter Street headquarters. Or talking to a counselor. Or visiting the on-site medical clinic. Or working at jobs arranged by Larkin—which for Bailey means cleaning offices at the Red and White Fleet [San Francisco's famous sightseeing tours] in addition to helping run Larkin's day laborer program. For Ononvakpuri, it means answering phones and writing newsletters at the Independent Living Skills Program.

Combinations of mental illness, crack addiction or physical abuse in their families threw both youths into the foster system, and for Bailey the fallout included minor drug and theft busts as a juvenile. Since they are both rebuilding relationships with their relatives, they didn't want extensive details printed. Just say it's "a challenge," they both said—such as when Bailey had to rescue his half-sister last month.

The key, both youths said, is to keep working for success. The Larkin program doesn't leave them much choice.

"They keep us busy," Bailey said, standing with Ononvakpuri at the Larkin office after a job-hunting seminar. "Which is good. I can't afford to waste time. I am applying to the California Culinary Academy. I am going to be a sous chef."

Ononvakpuri grinned. "You're already the only one who knows how to cook around here, so I'd say you're on your way," she said.

Ononvakpuri, who lived in homeless shelters with her mother as a little girl, just got accepted to UC Santa Cruz for the fall, and she intends to study creative writing. As she walked out of the Larkin office, she passed a homeless man sleeping in a pile of blankets on the sidewalk. Her face grew sad.

"I was always so afraid I'd turn out like that," she said quietly. "Thank God, I'm out of that. I am never going back."

One of her job counselors, Jesse Noonan, said she has no doubt. "It's all about attitude. Hers is awesome," she said.

Bailey gets a similar vote of confidence from his bosses at the Red and White Fleet.

"Kids his age so often talk back, but not Darnell," ticket agent Jozan Stevens said as she watched Bailey punch in for a shift. "He's lived a lot, but he's learned, you can tell. Does his job, stays friendly, stays clean. In a few years I see him with real money in his pocket." She raised her voice and added, "And no babies, right?" Bailey looked up and smiled, shaking his head.

"The boy has potential," Stevens said, beaming.

> "A whopping 25% to 40% of the home-
> less youth population in New York and
> other large American cities identify as
> lesbian, gay, bisexual, or transgender."

Homelessness Is a Serious Problem for Abandoned Gay Youths

Frank Mok

According to Frank Mok in the following viewpoint, gay youths, abandoned by their family or ostracized by their communities, often escape to urban areas. Having no resources, he asserts, many end up homeless. Some find their problems aggravated by rejection and abuse in homeless shelters, Mok maintains, and others turn to sex work, which may provide temporary shelter. Programs that increase acceptance of and find work for aban- doned gay youths, help many avoid homelessness, he claims. Mok writes on issues concerning gay youth for magazines such as the Advocate.

Frank Mok, "A Haven for Homeless Youths: Rejected by Family and Friends, Many Queer Youths Flee to the Streets of New York City. Amid Despair, Many Find Hope," *The Advocate*, issue 969, August 29, 2006, pp. 26–27. Copyright 2006 Frank Mok. Re- produced by permission.

As you read, consider the following questions:

1. As cited by the author, what did a 2003 New York City task force conclude about the homeless youth population in New York?
2. According to Mok, for every homeless youth who has a bed, how many are wandering the streets of New York?
3. Why is the lure of sex work so strong for homeless gay youth, in the author's opinion?

"Get out of our town, Satan!" That's what Kimy's peers said to her when she came out as a teenager in Utah. "They felt being gay was the same as being a child molester," 20-year-old Kimy, who eschews sexual identity labels but refers to herself as transgender, calmly explains. The hostility and intolerance Kimy endured from her family and hometown forced her to leave Utah at age 18 with few options. She ended up living on the streets of New York City.

That's where Tony Aguilar, a gay 20-year-old, ended up as well. When he came out to his mom in their Paterson, N.J., home at age 17, their relationship immediately changed. "We were best friends; we could've talked about anything," he recalls. "After I came out her attitude changed completely. Everything went bad." Then one day when he was 18, she told him to get his things and leave.

Fleeing to Urban Streets

Many abandoned queer youths find their way to urban centers, where they believe their chances of survival will be good. Once in the city, however, they quickly find out that making it is not as easy as they had hoped. Without support and resources, many are forced to live on the streets. According to a 2003 New York City task force report, numerous studies over the past decade have found that a whopping 25% to 40% of the homeless youth population in New York and other large American cities identify as lesbian, gay, bisexual, or transgender.

Services have been slow to address this population. According to the Interfaith Task Force for LGBTQ [lesbian, gay, bisexual, transgender, or questioning] Homeless Youth, there are only about 70 beds available for over 7,000 homeless LGBT youths in New York. For every homeless youth who has a bed, 99 others are spending their nights wandering the streets or sleeping on park benches, in subways, or on friends' couches. To survive, many resort to sex work, which sometimes gets them a bed at least for the night.

Everyone interviewed for this article reported having experienced long bouts of depression, and many have even attempted suicide in response to neglect. "I was tired all the time, and I wasn't eating either because I was depressed," says Tony. "I thought I wasn't gonna get nowhere."

To cope, many numb themselves to their situation. "I just block out my feelings," says Kristen Lovell, 24, a transgender woman from Yonkers, N.Y., whose mother kicked her out after reading her diary. "I just don't allow myself to feel anything."

Trouble at Traditional Shelters

Kimy eventually found herself at New York's Covenant House, which says it's the nation's largest shelter for homeless youth; it is the only one to receive New York City government funding. But once there, Kimy's situation didn't get better. "Covenant House doesn't like gay people, let me tell you," says Kimy, adding that her time there was "hell." She wasn't abused, something other LGBT youths who've stayed there have asserted, but fights occurred frequently. "The other kids would come into my room all the time and beat up my roommates," Kimy claims. When she complained, she says, the staff kicked her out.

"[The Covenant staff] would call me 'he/she' and 'faggot,'" says Michele Carver, a 19-year-old transgender woman from Georgia, who was kicked out of her home. "A friend told me about Ali Forney, so I went there."

The Risks of Homelessness Among Gay Youths

Studies have shown that a large segment—up to 38 percent—of homeless youth identify themselves as lesbian, gay, bisexual, trans-gender or "questioning." According to a 2001 report by the Chicago Coalition for the Homeless, they are more likely to be homeless as they face greater chances of violence at home, depression, suicide, and alcohol and drug abuse—all risk factors of homelessness. And they often leave home because of conflicts over their sexual orientation.

Amy Rainey, Chicago Reporter, *September/October 2005.*

Sheltering Homeless Gay Youths

The Ali Forney Center is one of only a handful of shelters, along with Sylvia's Place, Green Chimneys, Carmen's Place, and most recently, Trinity Place, offering beds to LGBT homeless youths in New York City; these agencies together shelter only about 1% of the city's homeless queer youth population. Rather than turn youths away, agencies such as Ali Forney try to provide them with options. "We try to find where there are vacancies at other shelters and to let the youths know they might not be safe at some of them," says Carl Siciliano, Ali Forney's executive director. "Given these choices some kids will choose to ride the subway trains all night rather than go to a shelter where they're likely to be harassed."

To increase awareness of the issue, Ali Forney has released a citywide ad campaign promoting its family counseling programs to help parents cope with having LGBT children. Each ad shows a child and parent with a tagline below them, "Would you stop loving [him/her] if you know [he's gay/she's lesbian]?" The Interfaith Task Force for LGBTQ Homeless Youth raised over $3,000 at a recent event.

These agencies also help homeless youth find work. "Where I'm from, you can't get a job being who I am," says Kimy. Michele agrees. "If I go to an interview as a woman, they say, 'We can't help you,' or 'The position is filled,' or 'Call back another time,'" she says. "And it's also hard to find a doctor who can take care of my medical needs."

A Continuing Struggle

Unable to find a job, the lure of sex work can be strong. Kristen, who was a messenger and waiter before her transition, is looking for regular work but continues to escort on the side. "It's hard because the streets have been good to me," she admits. "But now that I'm getting older, I need to stop."

Kimy is trying to get out of the cycle of being one step from the streets. "I have two hands and I have a brain, so I can do things for myself," she says.

However, the struggle continues. Kimy recently got an apartment with roommates and says she has even reconnected with her family back in Utah, noting that they speak to her regularly and plan to visit her in New York sometime. But when she tried to go back to Utah to live on her own, it didn't work out, so she had to return to Sylvia's Place. She has two jobs: one as a tour guide in Times Square and the other as an intern with a fashion designer, a position she got through Sylvia's Place. Despite her recent hardships, "a lot of people in New York really believe in me, and that makes me feel really good about myself," she says.

Kimy can be considered lucky: Tony and Kristen have little or no relationship with their respective families, although they would like to. For now they are focused on other goals. Kristen, who spends nights at Sylvia's Place, plans to save money and find a place to live, go through with her transition, and get a college degree. Tony, who's at the Ali Forney Center, says he wants to go to college to become a pediatrician. Michele, who talks with her grandmother almost daily, considered joining Job Corps, a federally funded job training and educational program, but changed her mind. . . . She ha[s] left her housing to strike out on her own.

"It's hard, but I've not given up hope, because there's still faith for all [homeless queer youth] out there," Michele says. "It'll get a whole lot better. This is only the beginning."

Periodical Bibliography

The following articles have been selected to supplement the diverse views presented in this chapter.

Jessica L. Aberle "Homelessness Not Just an 'Urban Problem,'" *Peoria (IL) Journal Star*, June 4, 2006.

Herbert R. Bennett "Speaking Out for Homeless Kids," *New York Times Upfront*, November 28, 2005.

Issues & Controversies on File "Homelessness," *Issues & Controversies @ FACTS.com*, September 25, 2006.

Michelle Kennedy "What I Couldn't Say Out Loud: I Am Homeless," *Redbook*, April 2005.

Will La Page "Homeless and Hopeless in the Park," *Parks & Recreation*, August 2005.

Los Angeles Times "Housing Homeless Families," June 12, 2006.

Kellie Lunney "Crash Course in Homelessness," *National Journal*, November 5, 2005.

National Coalition for the Homeless "Who Is Homeless?" *NCH Fact Sheet*, June 2006.

Alexandra Marks "Back from Iraq—and Suddenly Out on the Streets," *Christian Science Monitor*, February 8, 2005.

Barbara Rahder "The Crisis of Women's Homelessness in Canada: Summary of the CERA Report," *Women & Environments International Magazine*, Spring 2006.

Amy Rainey "Seeking Acceptance: Clashes at Home over Sexual Orientation Are Pushing Many Young Adults to the Streets," *Chicago Reporter*, September/October 2005.

Leo Shane "Advocates See Veterans of War on Terror Joining the Ranks of the Homeless," *Stars & Stripes*, June 3, 2005.

OPPOSING
VIEWPOINTS®
SERIES

CHAPTER 2

What Factors Contribute to Homelessness?

Chapter Preface

In 2004 roughly 45.8 million Americans—15.7 percent of the U.S. population—had no health care insurance. In fact, many advocates for the homeless claim, a lack of adequate health insurance puts millions of American adults and children one accident or illness away from homelessness. High medical bills make it difficult for many to pay for food, utilities, or rent. While most homeless activists cite a lack of affordable housing and poverty as the primary factors that contribute to homelessness, many claim a lack of affordable health care itself plays a significant role in the persistence of homelessness in the United States.

One reason that a lack of affordable health care contributes to homelessness is that the uninsured often do not seek preventative care. For those who finally do seek care in cases of emergency or severe illness, health care costs are much higher, and many are forced to face the difficult choice between paying medical bills or housing costs. "For a single working mom with one or two children, even a minor childhood illness can mean a long wait in a neighborhood health clinic or hospital emergency room for free care," Horizons for Homeless Children claims. Rather than miss work, single mothers and others without health insurance often wait until health problems are serious and care is costly, creating a significant financial burden. The Kaiser Commission on Medicaid and the Uninsured reports that 44 percent of the uninsured had a difficult time paying medical bills in 2002. Because inadequate use of medical care can lead to poor health, the commission asserts, it can also affect the ability to work or go to school. "Lower productivity and inadequate education," the commission claims, "reduce earnings and put individuals at risk for homelessness."

A reduction in employer-based health insurance is another reason for the connection between inadequate health care and homelessness. A common misconception, claims the Chicago Coalition for the Homeless (CCH), is that the uninsured are unemployed. "In reality," CCH contends, "more than 80 percent of uninsured children and adults under the age of 65 live in working families." Many workers have service jobs that "often do not provide insurance," CCH maintains, "and the low wages make accessing coverage difficult even when an employer does offer it." In addition, analysts assert, a poor economy has forced some employers who once offered health care benefits to cut these programs. "The recession has shown us that employer-sponsored health insurance cannot always be protected when the economy suffers and premiums rise dramatically," CCH asserts. "Workers who earn low wages," CCH argues, "are increasingly at risk of losing housing and jobs when this occurs." Adding to the problem, these advocates argue, are the economic crises faced by many federal, state, and local governments. Many have been forced to eliminate rather than expand health care benefits for the poor. Advocates for the homeless argue that governments must nevertheless place a higher priority on providing health benefits to prevent homelessness. According to CCH, "health insurance and healthcare are human rights. It is imperative that we create a system that offers an affordable healthcare safety net that is available to all individuals."

The relationship between a lack of affordable health care and homelessness remains controversial. The authors in the following chapter express their views on the factors they believe contribute to homelessness and the implications for homelessness policy.

| "Homelessness results from a complex set of circumstances that require people to choose between food, shelter, and other basic needs."

Multiple Factors Contribute to Homelessness

National Coalition for the Homeless

A variety of factors contribute to homelessness, argues the National Coalition for the Homeless (NCH) in the following viewpoint. Poverty and a lack of affordable housing are the primary risk factors, the coalition claims. Indeed, low wages and a decline in public assistance make it difficult for poor families who must pay rising housing costs, especially those who must also pay for expensive health care, NCH maintains. Also at risk are those who suffer from mental illness, addiction, and domestic violence, NCH asserts. NCH is an advocacy organization working to end homelessness.

As you read, consider the following questions:

1. In the opinion of NCH, what factors contribute to wage declines?

2. According to the author, what explains declining welfare rolls?

National Coalition for the Homeless, "NCH Fact Sheet #1: Why Are People Homeless?" June 2006. Reproduced by permission.

3. What did the 2003 U.S. Department of Health and Human Services Report, as cited by the author, reveal about the mentally ill homeless?

Two trends are largely responsible for the rise in homelessness over the past 20–25 years: a growing shortage of affordable rental housing and a simultaneous increase in poverty. Below is an overview of . . . poverty and housing statistics, as well as additional factors contributing to homelessness. . . .

The Link Between Homelessness and Poverty

Homelessness and poverty are inextricably linked. Poor people are frequently unable to pay for housing, food, childcare, health care, and education. Difficult choices must be made when limited resources cover only some of these necessities. Often it is housing, which absorbs a high proportion of income, that must be dropped. Being poor means being an illness, an accident, or a paycheck away from living on the streets.

In 2004, 12.7% of the U.S. population, or 37 million people, lived in poverty. Both the poverty rate and the number of poor people have increased in recent years, up from 12.5% in 2003, and up 1.1 million from 2003 (U.S. Bureau of the Census, 2005). 36% of persons living in poverty are children; in fact, the 2004 poverty rate of 17.6% for children under 18 years old is significantly higher than the poverty rate for any other age group.

Two factors help account for increasing poverty: eroding employment opportunities for large segments of the workforce, and the declining value and availability of public assistance.

Eroding Work Opportunities

Media reports of a growing economy and low unemployment mask a number of important reasons why homelessness persists, and, in some areas of the country, is worsening. These reasons include stagnant or falling incomes and less secure jobs which offer fewer benefits.

While the last few years have seen growth in real wages at all levels, these increases have not been enough to counteract a long pattern of stagnant and declining wages. Low-wage workers have been particularly hard hit by wage trends and have been left behind as the disparity between rich and poor has mushroomed. To compound the problem, the real value of the minimum wage in 2004 was 26% less than in 1979. Although incomes appear to be rising, this growth is largely due to more hours worked—which in turn can be attributed to welfare reform and the tight labor markets. Factors contributing to wage declines include a steep drop in the number and bargaining power of unionized workers; erosion in the value of the minimum wage; a decline in manufacturing jobs and the corresponding expansion of lower-paying service-sector employment; globalization; and increased nonstandard work, such as temporary and part-time employment.

Declining wages, in turn, have put housing out of reach for many workers: in every state, more than the minimum wage is required to afford a one- or two-bedroom apartment at Fair Market Rent. A . . . U.S. Conference of Mayors report stated that in every state more than the minimum-wage is required to afford a one or two-bedroom apartment at 30% of his or her income, which is the federal definition of affordable housing. In 2001, five million rental households had "worst case housing needs," which means that they paid more than half their incomes for rent, living in severely substandard housing, or both. The primary source of income for 80% of these households was earnings from jobs.

Work Is No Escape from Poverty

The connection between impoverished workers and homelessness can be seen in homeless shelters, many of which house significant numbers of full-time wage earners. A survey of 24 U.S. cities found that 15% of persons in homeless situations are employed. Surveys in past years have yielded the percentage of homeless working to be as high as 26%. In a number of cities not surveyed by the U.S. Conference of Mayors—as well as in many states—the percentage is even higher.

The future of job growth does not appear promising for many workers: a 1998 study estimated that 46% of the jobs with the most growth between 1994 and 2005 pay less than $16,000 a year; these jobs will not lift families out of poverty. Morever, 74% of these jobs pay below a livable wage ($32,185 for a family of four).

Thus, for many Americans, work provides no escape from poverty. The benefits of economic growth have not been equally distributed; instead, they have been concentrated at the top of income and wealth distributions. A rising tide does not lift all boats, and in the United States today, many boats are struggling to stay afloat.

A Decline in Public Assistance

The declining value and availability of public assistance is another source of increasing poverty and homelessness. Until its repeal in August 1996, the largest cash assistance program for poor families with children was the Aid to Families with Dependent Children (AFDC) program. The Personal Responsibility and Work Opportunity Reconciliation Act of 1996 (the federal welfare reform law) repealed the AFDC program and replaced it with a block grant program called Temporary Assistance to Needy Families (TANF). Current TANF benefits and Food Stamps combined are below the poverty level in every state; in fact, the current maximum TANF benefit for a single mother of two children is 29% of the federal poverty level. Thus, contrary to popular opinion, welfare does not provide relief from poverty.

Welfare caseloads have dropped sharply since the passage and implementation of welfare reform legislation. However, declining welfare rolls simply mean that fewer people are receiving benefits—not that they are employed or doing better financially. Early findings suggest that although more families are moving from welfare to work, many of them are faring poorly due to low wages and inadequate work supports. Only a small fraction of welfare recipients' new jobs pay above-poverty wages; most of the new jobs pay far below the poverty line. . . .

Moreover, extreme poverty is growing more common for children, especially those in female-headed and working families. This increase can be traced directly to the declining number of children lifted above one-half of the poverty line by government cash assistance for the poor.

As a result of loss of benefits, low wages, and unstable employment, many families leaving welfare struggle to get medical care, food, and housing. Many lose health insurance, despite continued Medicaid eligibility: a study found that 675,000 people lost health insurance in 1997 as a result of the federal welfare reform legislation, including 400,000 children. Moreover, over 725,000 workers, laid off from their jobs due to the recession in 2000, lost their health insurance. According to the Children's Defense Fund, over nine million children in America have no health insurance, and over 90 percent of them are in working families.

The Impact of Reducing Benefits

In addition, housing is rarely affordable for families leaving welfare for low wages, yet subsidized housing is so limited that fewer than one in four TANF families nationwide lives in public housing or receives a housing voucher to help them rent a private unit. For most families leaving the rolls, housing subsidies are not an option. In some communities, former welfare families appear to be experiencing homelessness in increasing numbers.

In addition to the reduction in the value and availability of welfare benefits for families, recent policy changes have reduced or eliminated public assistance for poor, single individuals. Several states have cut or eliminated General Assistance (GA) benefits for single impoverished people, despite evidence that the availability of GA reduces the prevalence of homelessness.

People with disabilities, too, must struggle to obtain and maintain stable housing. In 1998, on a national average, a person receiving Supplemental Security Income (SSI) benefits had to spend 69% of his or her SSI monthly income to rent a one-bedroom apartment at Fair Market Rent; in more than 125 housing market areas, the cost of a one-bedroom apartment at Fair Market Rent was more than a person's total monthly SSI income. Today, only nine percent of non-institutionalized people receiving SSI receive housing assistance.

Presently, most states have not replaced the old welfare system with an alternative that enables families and individuals to obtain above-poverty employment and to sustain themselves when work is not available or possible.

The Housing Problem

A lack of affordable housing and the limited scale of housing assistance programs have contributed to the current housing crisis and to homelessness.

The gap between the number of affordable housing units and the number of people needing them has created a housing crisis for poor people. Between 1973 and 1993, 2.2 million low-rent units disappeared from the market. These units were either abandoned, converted into condominiums or expensive apartments, or became unaffordable because of cost increases. Between 1991 and 1995, median rental costs paid by low-income renters rose 21%; at the same time, the number of low-income renters increased. Over these years, despite an im-

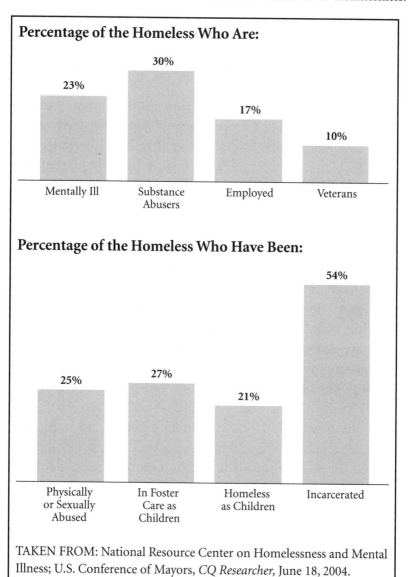

Percentage of the Homeless Who Are:

30%

23%

17%

10%

Mentally Ill   Substance   Employed   Veterans
Abusers

Percentage of the Homeless Who Have Been:

54%

25%

27%

21%

Physically   In Foster   Homeless   Incarcerated
or Sexually   Care as   as Children
Abused   Children

TAKEN FROM: National Resource Center on Homelessness and Mental Illness; U.S. Conference of Mayors, *CQ Researcher,* June 18, 2004.

proving economy, the affordable housing gap grew by one million. Between 1970 and 1995, the gap between the number of low-income renters and the amount of affordable housing units skyrocketed from a nonexistent gap to a shortage of 4.4 million affordable housing units—the largest shortfall on record. According to HUD [Housing and Urban Development], . . . the shortages of affordable housing are most severe for units affordable to renters with extremely low incomes. Federal support for low-income housing has fallen 49% from 1980 to 2003. . . .

The strong economy has caused rents to soar, putting housing out of reach for the poorest Americans. After the 1980s, income growth has never kept pace with rents, and since 2000, the incomes of low-income households has declined as rents continue to rise. The number of housing units that rent for less than $300, adjusted for inflation, declined from 6.8 million in 1996 to 5.5 million in 1998, a 19 percent drop of 1.3 million units. The loss of affordable housing puts even greater numbers of people at risk of homelessness.

The lack of affordable housing has led to high rent burdens (rents which absorb a high proportion of income), overcrowding, and substandard housing. These phenomena, in turn, have not only forced many people to become homeless; they have put a large and growing number of people at risk of becoming homeless. A 2001 Housing and Urban Development (HUD) study found that 4.9 million unassisted, very low-income households—this is 10.9 million people, 3.6 million of whom are children—had "worst case needs" for housing assistance in 1999. Although this figure seems to be a decrease from 1997, it is misleading since, in the same two-year span, "the number of units affordable to extremely low-income renters dropped between 1997 and 1999 at an accelerated rate, and shortages of housing both affordable and available to these renters actually worsened."

A Need for Housing Assistance

Housing assistance can make the difference between stable housing, precarious housing, or no housing at all. However, the demand for assisted housing clearly exceeds the supply: only about one-third of poor renter households receive a housing subsidy from the federal, state, or local government.

The limited level of housing assistance means that most poor families and individuals seeking housing assistance are placed on long waiting lists. From 1996–1998, the time households spent on waiting lists for HUD housing assistance grew dramatically. For the largest public housing authorities, a family's average time on a waiting list rose from 22 to 33 months from 1996 to 1998—a 50% increase. The average waiting period for a Section 8 rental assistance voucher rose from 26 months to 28 months between 1996 and 1998. Today the average wait for Section 8 Vouchers is 35 months.

Excessive waiting lists for public housing mean that people must remain in shelters or inadequate housing arrangements longer. For instance, in the mid-1990s in New York, families stayed in a shelter an average of five months before moving on to permanent housing. In a survey of 24 cities, people remain homeless an average of seven months, and 87% of cities reported that the length of time people are homeless has increased. . . . Longer stays in homeless shelters result in less shelter space available for other homeless people, who must find shelter elsewhere or live on the streets. . . .

Other Contributing Factors

Particularly within the context of poverty and the lack of affordable housing, certain additional factors may push people into homelessness. Other major factors, which can contribute to homelessness, include the following:

Lack of Affordable Health Care For families and individuals struggling to pay the rent, a serious illness or disability can start a downward spiral into homelessness, beginning with a lost job, depletion of savings to pay for care, and eventual eviction. In 2004, approximately 45.8 million Americans had no health care insurance. That equates to 15.7% of the population. Nearly a third of persons living in poverty had no health insurance of any kind. The coverage held by many others would not carry them through a catastrophic illness.

Domestic Violence Battered women who live in poverty are often forced to choose between abusive relationships and homelessness. In a study of 777 homeless parents (the majority of whom were mothers) in ten U.S. cities, 22% said they had left their last place of residence because of domestic violence. In addition, 50% of the cities surveyed by the U.S. Conference of Mayors identified domestic violence as a primary cause of homelessness. Studying the entire country, though, reveals that the problem is even more serious. Nationally, approximately half of all women and children experiencing homelessness are fleeing domestic violence.

Mental Illness Approximately 22% of the single adult homeless population suffers from some form of severe and persistent mental illnesses. Despite the disproportionate number of severely mentally ill people among the homeless population, increases in homelessness are not attributable to the release of severely mentally ill people from institutions. Most patients were released from mental hospitals in the 1950s and 1960s, yet vast increases in homelessness did not occur until the 1980s, when incomes and housing options for those living on the margins began to diminish rapidly. According to the 2003 U.S. Department of Health and Human Services Report, most homeless persons with mental illness do not need to be institutionalized, but can live in the community with the appropriate supportive housing options. However, many mentally ill homeless people are unable to obtain access to supportive housing and/or other treatment services. The mental health support services most needed include case management, housing, and treatment.

Addiction Disorders The relationship between addiction and homelessness is complex and controversial. While rates of alcohol and drug abuse are disproportionately high among the homeless population, the increase in homelessness over the past two decades cannot be explained by addiction alone.

Many people who are addicted to alcohol and drugs never become homeless, but people who are poor and addicted are clearly at increased risk of homelessness. During the 1980s, competition for increasingly scarce low-income housing grew so intense that those with disabilities such as addiction and mental illness were more likely to lose out and find themselves on the streets. The loss of SRO [single room occupancy] housing, a source of stability for many poor people suffering from addiction and/or mental illness, was a major factor in increased homelessness in many communities.

Addiction does increase the risk of displacement for the precariously housed; in the absence of appropriate treatment, it may doom one's chances of getting housing once on the streets. Homeless people often face insurmountable barriers to obtaining health care, including addictive disorder treatment services and recovery supports. The following are among the obstacles to treatment for homeless persons: lack of health insurance; lack of documentation; waiting lists; scheduling difficulties; daily contact requirements; lack of transportation; ineffective treatment methods; lack of supportive services; and cultural insensitivity. An in-depth study of 13 communities across the nation revealed service gaps in every community in at least one stage of the treatment and recovery continuum for homeless people.

Homelessness results from a complex set of circumstances that require people to choose between food, shelter, and other basic needs. Only a concerted effort to ensure jobs that pay a living wage, adequate support for those who cannot work, affordable housing, and access to health care will bring an end to homelessness.

> "Drug and alcohol abuse is a major contributing factor toward an individual's vulnerability to homelessness."

Substance Abuse Contributes to Homelessness

Diana Mahoney

According to Diana Mahoney in the following viewpoint, 30 percent of America's chronic homeless are substance abusers. While proving a clear causal relationship between substance abuse and homelessness is difficult, she argues, a significant number of the substance abusing homeless in one study had abused substances before they became homeless. Because the relationship between substance abuse and homelessness remains unclear, Mahoney claims, policy makers debate whether treatment or housing should come first. Mahoney writes for Clinical Psychiatry News, *an independent newspaper for psychiatrists.*

As you read, consider the following questions:

1. According to Mahoney, what additional factors increase the vulnerability of substance abusers?

2. In the author's opinion, what is the alternative to the difficult task of treating both problems of the substance abusing homeless?

Diana Mahoney, "Addressing Homelessness and Substance Abuse," *Clinical Psychiatry News*, vol. 34, no. 3, March 2006, p. 56. Copyright 2006 International Medical News Group. Reproduced by permission.

3. What does Mahoney claim was the result of a study contrasting housing- and multiple treatment-first programs in New York City?

Of the estimated 3 million people in the United States who are homeless during the course of a year, about 30% are chronic substance abusers, according to the U.S. Conference of Mayors.

Most experts agree that the actual numbers are probably much higher.

For example, in one survey of more than 500 homeless adults at nearly 100 sites across Pittsburgh and Philadelphia, about 78% of the respondents met DSM-III-R [the *Diagnostic and Statistical Manual of Mental Disorders,* 3rd ed., a handbook used in diagnosing mental disorders] criteria for substance abuse, dependence on alcohol or drugs, or a combination of both, with the most common substances of abuse being alcohol, cocaine, and heroin.

The co-occurrence of substance abuse and homelessness makes sense. The realities of homelessness impede consistent participation in substance abuse interventions and continued engagement in treatment strategies. Similarly, chronic substance abuse often limits social and familial ties, prevents gainful employment, and drains financial resources.

It is clear that substance abuse and homelessness often go hand in hand, but what is less clear is which condition precipitates the other—and how to intervene in a way that addresses both problems.

Looking at the Evidence

In a cross-sectional study of 900 homeless individuals that looked at temporal relationships between relative onset of mental illness and homelessness, investigators from Washington University in St. Louis determined that nearly 88% of the homeless men and 84% of the homeless women who abused

The Relationship Between Chronic Homelessness and Substance Abuse

There is a clear relationship between chronic homelessness and substance abuse in the United States. Addiction precipitates and sustains homelessness. It also inhibits one's ability to work and destroys families and other social relationships. Consequently, once an abuser loses his or her source of income and housing, friends or family may be unwilling to offer assistance. In an increasingly competitive affordable housing market, drug and alcohol abusers are the last to qualify for housing benefits and thus end up on the streets more than the rest of the low-income population. Additionally, new welfare and Social Security Disability income regulations concerning alcohol and drug abusers severely limit, and in most cases, eliminate this group's eligibility for such assistance.

San Diego Regional Task Force on the Homeless,
"Substance Abuse and Homelessness," www.rtfhsd.org.

alcohol had been diagnosed with an alcohol use disorder in the year before becoming homeless. Similarly, for drug abuse, 78% of men and 69% of women were diagnosed with a drug use disorder in the year before becoming homeless.

These findings suggest a causative relationship between substance abuse and homelessness. But the authors point out that not every alcoholic or drug abuser becomes homeless. Thus, it can only be said that drug and alcohol abuse is a major contributing factor toward an individual's vulnerability to homelessness. Other factors that increase vulnerability include poverty, poor employment, lack of education, and a history of abuse or neglect, according to David E. Pollio, Ph.D., one of the study's authors.

Looking at the impact of homelessness on substance abuse also precludes definitive cause-and-effect explanations. In the two-city Pennsylvania study, for example, homelessness increased self-reported substance abuse in 30% of the respondents who had substance abuse problems. The remaining 70% reported that their substance abuse stayed at the same level or decreased after they became homeless.

Among those who reported an increase in their substance abuse when they became homeless, "the increase was often in response to self-reported mental health symptoms" such as anxiety or depression, according to the authors.

A Complex Relationship

Whether homelessness begets substance abuse or vice versa, the findings of these and other studies suggest a complex relationship. The prospect of addressing both conditions is daunting, but the alternative is to continue to pour money, time, and resources into programs that are almost doomed.

Just how to address both conditions has been the subject of much debate. Some experts favor the "treatment first" approach, whereby treatment adherence and abstinence are prerequisites to housing. Others advocate for "housing first" interventions. Under this approach, clients are housed and provided immediate case management services and treatment access.

It has been proposed that not making treatment adherence a prerequisite to housing minimizes client incentives to become or stay clean, and in so doing dilutes the intervention. But a New York University School of Social Work study suggests otherwise.

The investigators analyzed data from 225 homeless adults in New York City involved in a longitudinal experiment contrasting a housing-first program and multiple treatment-first programs. After 48 months, "there were no significant group differences in alcohol and drug use," the authors wrote. These findings "show that 'dual diagnosed' adults can remain stably housed without increasing their substance use."

Another approach under investigation in Alabama may be more successful than either the housing-first or treatment-first programs.

Importantly, the federal government is taking notice of the plight of homeless people suffering from substance abuse disorders. [In 2005], the Department of Housing and Urban Development distributed $10 million in grants through a new "Housing for People Who Are Homeless and Addicted to Alcohol" initiative. Ten U.S. cities received funding for innovative projects that link substance abuse treatment for homeless persons to housing and other wraparound service needs.

The next step will be to move the most promising projects into practice.

> *"About a quarter to a third of the homeless have a serious mental illness—usually schizophrenia, bipolar disorder, or severe depression—and the proportion is growing."*

The Mentally Ill Are Vulnerable to Homelessness

Harvard Mental Health Letter

A significant number of America's homeless suffer from mental illness, claims the Harvard Mental Health Letter *in the following viewpoint. The mentally ill are more vulnerable to homelessness, the author asserts, because without help they are unable to negotiate the complex processes of finding housing and of protecting themselves from eviction. Once homeless, the author argues, many feel threatened by the shelter environment, and housing without complementary mental health services is not likely to help. The* Harvard Mental Health Letter *is a monthly newsletter exploring current thinking and debate on mental health issues.*

As you read, consider the following questions:

1. According to the *Harvard Mental Health Letter*, why do many mentally ill homeless avoid shelters?
2. According to the author, what group of mentally ill people are at an especially high risk of homelessness?
3. Against what group of people is discrimination legal, according to the author?

Hundreds of thousands of Americans spend the night in shelters or on the streets, and a high proportion of them have serious mental illnesses. How this situation has come about and how to change it are questions that concern the general public as well as mental health professionals. There are signs that the beginning of a solution may be emerging.

About 600,000 people are homeless on any given night, and 2 million at some time in any given year. Over a five-year period, 2%–3% of the population, as many as 8 million people, will be homeless for at least one night. Of these, 80% find a home within a few weeks, but about 10% remain homeless for a year or more. The United States Department of Health and Human Services estimates the number of chronically homeless at 100,000–200,000.

About a quarter to a third of the homeless have a serious mental illness—usually schizophrenia, bipolar disorder, or severe depression—and the proportion is growing. A study published [in 2004] . . . showed a 20-year rise in the rate of psychiatric illness among the homeless in St. Louis. In the year 2000, 30% had a combination of mental health and drug or alcohol problems (dual diagnosis) and another 15% had mental health problems alone. A survey of more than 10,000 patients treated for serious mental illness in San Diego County found that 15% had been homeless during the previous year.

The main sources of support for the homeless are Social Security provided by the federal government and emergency public shelters, mostly operated by voluntary lay groups or religious organizations. Shelters are often filthy, dangerous, and crime-ridden. There is little privacy and staff members frequently have no specialized training. Many of the mentally ill avoid shelters because they fear violence and theft or cannot tolerate the noise, crowds, and confusion.

Chronic homelessness is often the latest chapter in a story that begins in childhood. One study of first-time applicants to homeless shelters with histories of psychiatric hospitalization found that half of them had been institutionalized or placed in foster care as children. They become homeless when there is a crisis—their families can no longer live with them, their rent is raised, they are discharged from a prison or psychiatric hospital. Poor family support, a history of lawbreaking, and especially alcohol or drug addiction are major factors.

The mentally ill and people addicted to alcohol or drugs are the first victims of housing shortages. Many of the poor are in danger of losing their homes when their income falls or rent increases. In these circumstances the mentally ill—many of whom pay more than half their income for housing—are most likely to be evicted because their disabilities make it difficult for others to help or even tolerate them. Once they are on the streets, their isolation becomes more serious, because lost connections are difficult to re-establish.

Mentally ill people who have been in jail or prison are at especially high risk of homelessness. They find it difficult to negotiate the complex process of regaining the entitlements they have lost after incarceration. They have to wait for resumption of their Social Security benefits at a time when they may already have been evicted. Their criminal records make it especially difficult to get housing.

Housing

Housing programs are complex, competitive, and difficult to access for people with mental illness, especially those with a dual diagnosis. Landlords and neighbors don't want them.

Much of the housing available to them does not meet federal standards that would allow them to receive rent subsidies.

Some housing choices are a good match for the mentally ill homeless, though resources are limited. Transitional housing is a group home in which patients learn the skills they need to live independently, with non-professional staff on-site 24 hours a day. Supportive housing consists of a number of rental apartments in one location with 24-hour crisis support services on-site. Supported housing, usually individual apartments not all in one location, provides more flexible 24-hour off-site support and crisis services. The distinction between supported and supportive housing is not always precise, and there are many intermediate variations.

Most of the mentally ill say they do not want to live in groups with other mentally ill people. They prefer a family home or supported or supportive housing. They would like to be able to call for help when they need it, but they are less enthusiastic about rehabilitation services that make demands and create expectations—although once they are housed, they may become more amenable to that kind of support.

Studies have shown that because of savings elsewhere in the system, providing housing for the mentally ill does not even necessarily increase costs. One study found that homeless persons placed in supportive housing spent 57% fewer days in psychiatric hospitals, made 58% fewer visits to emergency rooms, and had a 50% lower rate of imprisonment. A University of Pennsylvania study found that homeless people with mental illnesses placed in permanent supportive housing cost the public $16,000 less per year for emergency room services, jails, and psychiatric hospitalization. Another study comparing comprehensive housing services with case management alone found that housing was particularly useful for people with severe psychiatric symptoms and serious substance abuse problems.

Important as housing is, it cannot solve all the problems of the homeless mentally ill, and many will not even be able to remain in the housing provided for them unless they also receive psychiatric treatment and other services. Often too depressed or disorganized to seek help for themselves, they confront a poorly coordinated system in which mental health, general health, housing, alcohol treatment, drug treatment, and legal services are all provided by separate agencies with unclear responsibities, high staff turnover, poor communication, and complex and sometimes mutually contradictory rules. The federal government alone operates 42 programs serving people with mental illness, of which the two largest are SSI (Supplemental Security Income) and SSDI (Social Security Disability Insurance). Other federal programs involve medical care, child welfare, criminal justice, education, rehabilitation, and drug and alcohol treatment.

A special problem is that although discrimination against the disabled in general is illegal, discrimination against users of illicit drugs and alcohol abusers is not. Landlords can refuse to rent to them, housing programs can exclude them, and group homes and supportive housing can reject them. But demanding abstinence from drugs or alcohol before housing and services are provided is usually asking too much of the mentally ill homeless.

Integrating Services

Combining services in a rational way is one of the most important unmet needs. Federal agencies have to be more flexible in supporting community practices that integrate services. Mental illness and substance abuse programs must be better coordinated with one another and with housing. Under consideration are service centers that deal with many problems and treatment teams that employ several professions.

A Tragic Side Effect of Non-treatment

Approximately 200,000 individuals with schizoprenia or manic-depressive illness are homeless, constituting one-third of the approximately 600,000 homeless population (total homeless population statistic based on data from Department of Health and Human Services). These 200,000 individuals comprise more than the entire population of many U.S. cities. . . .

At any given time, there are more people with untreated severe psychiatric illnesses living on America's streets than are receiving care in hospitals. Approximately 90,000 individuals with schizophrenia or manic-depressive illness are in hospitals receiving treatment for their disease.

In many cities such as New York, these people are now an accepted part of the urban landscape and make up a significant percentage of the homeless who ride subways all night, sleep on sidewalks, or sleep in the parks. These ill individuals drift into the train and bus stations, and even the airports.

Treatment Advocacy Center,
www.psychlaws.org.

One effective form of system integration is the use of case managers, agents who serve as advocates for the homeless, help them plan and monitor treatment, escort them to appointments, represent them in hearings, and generally help them make their way through the bureaucracy.

Another aspect of integration is outreach—workers who go to the homeless where they live instead of waiting for a crisis or a specific demand. The outreach program known as assertive community treatment consists of teams of professionals and others who provide help to the mentally ill on the streets and in shelters.

Access

The federally supported demonstration program, Access to Community Care and Effective Services and Supports (ACCESS), ran from 1993 to 1998 as an experiment in system integration. The government provided funds to enhance outreach and case management for the homeless at 18 sites in 9 states. In each state, one community was also given additional funds for system integration. After the funding ended, 17 of the sites continued some of the services with new funding.

The program succeeded in drawing hard-to-reach homeless people into community health services and sometimes housing. A three-year analysis of its effects among 146 participants in Pennsylvania found that they used more psychiatric care during and after the program, while spending fewer days in psychiatric hospitals. Another study examined living arrangements among 5,000 formerly homeless people a year after they received intensive case management in the ACCESS program. Only 11% had been homeless during the previous 30 days.

Another model program, legislated in California, is Integrated Services for Homeless Adults with Serious Mental Illness. Its purpose is to do whatever is necessary to meet the needs of the homeless wherever they are, offering a broad array of services, including outreach, 24-hour availability of help, and ongoing evaluation. There are no eligibility requirements, and the funding is flexible. Participants have a greatly decreased rate of imprisonment and psychiatric hospitalization as well as 80% fewer days of homelessness.

Critical Time Intervention is a successful program originally designed for homeless mothers with dual diagnosis who were released from jails or psychiatric hospitals. It includes transitional housing, intensive case management for nine months, and integrated treatment for the mental illness and substance abuse.

More research is needed on ways to bring the homeless into permanent housing and on which kinds of service delivery and physical accommodations are best. But we already know most of what has to be done. Some authorities are now saying that the mentally ill in the community should be provided with most or all of the services they would receive in a psychiatric hospital. Insurance and other reimbursement arrangements that discriminate against the chronic mentally ill have to be changed. Financing, including Medicare and Medicaid, must be adequate for their needs. Funding for medical and psychiatric treatment should be coordinated with funding for income support, social services, and housing.

Continuous care should be assured by more effective case management, outreach, and some form of critical time intervention. State Medicaid agencies will have to provide more funding for services like assertive community treatment, supported employment, and integrated dual diagnosis treatment. The choice of programs should be made at the local level as much as possible (at present, the states make most decisions about allocating funds, using block grants from the federal government).

Better discharge planning in psychiatric hospitals and prisons is especially important. Patients and prisoners about to be discharged should have housing arrangements, a treatment plan, medication if necessary, an appointment with a mental health professional, and an application for public income assistance. A ruling of the United States Supreme Court may help to bring about change. The Court [in *Olmstead v. L.C.* (1999)] has determined that states may be violating the discrimination provisions of the Americans with Disabilities Act if the discharge policies of state psychiatric hospitals result directly in homelessness.

The evidence that homelessness is expensive for society— and the apparent cost-effectiveness of programs aimed at reducing it—have inspired thoughts of ending it for good. Several cities, including Seattle and Boston, have explicitly committed themselves to that goal, and President [George W. Bush] has announced a 10-year effort to end chronic homelessness. The New Freedom Commission on Mental Health recommended in its 2004 report to the President that the Department of Housing and Urban Development develop a program to provide 150,000 units of permanent supportive housing for chronically homeless people.

Whether promises will be kept and good intentions realized is still doubtful; for example, [the 2005] federal budget includes a severe cut in funds for supportive housing. Homelessness is one symptom of a public mental health system in trouble. After adjustment for inflation, states now spend 30% less on mental health care than they did in 1955. Medicaid funding for psychiatric treatment is so low that private practitioners are refusing to accept insurance payments, clinics are closing, hospitals are reducing the number of beds reserved for psychiatric patients, and psychiatric emergency room visits are on the rise. [The 2004] report of the New Freedom Commission, while calling for measures to end homelessness, recommends a "fundamental transformation in the American system of mental health care" and implies that the needs of the homeless will never be fully met until all of the seriously mentally ill receive care of a quality that is rarely available to them now.

| *"For years, advocates have known that domestic violence is a primary cause of homelessness for women and families."*

Domestic Violence Often Leads to Homelessness

American Civil Liberties Union Foundation

In the following viewpoint the American Civil Liberties Union Foundation argues that domestic violence is a principal cause of homelessness for women and families. Abused women, controlled and isolated by their abusers, have little access to money or friends and family who can help them escape violent relationships, the foundation maintains. Compounding the problem, the foundation asserts, are landlords who often refuse to rent to abused women and evict victims who reveal that they are being abused. To help women and their children escape abusive homes, federal laws must end discrimination against domestic violence victims, the author reasons.

As you read, consider the following questions:

1. What did a fair housing group in New York City find when it contacted housing providers about a survivor assistance program, according to the author?

American Civil Liberties Union Foundation, "Women's Rights Project Fact Sheet: Domestic Violence and Homelessness," March 21, 2006. Copyright © 2006 ACLU, 125 Broad Street, 18th Floor, New York, NY 10004. Reproduced by permission.

2. According to the foundation, why are poor women more vulnerable to homelessness?

3. In what public housing assistance program has discrimination against domestic violence victims been prohibited, according to the author?

When women flee domestic abuse, they are often forced to leave their homes, with nowhere else to turn. Landlords also sometimes turn victims of domestic violence out of their homes because of the violence against them. For years, advocates have known that domestic violence is a primary cause of homelessness for women and families. Studies from across the country confirm the connection between domestic violence and homelessness and suggest ways to end the cycle in which violence against women leads to life on the streets.

Trapped Between Violence and Homelessness

Housing instability and a lack of safe and affordable housing options heightens the risks for women experiencing domestic violence.

A lack of alternative housing often leads women to stay in or return to violent relationships. In Minnesota in 2003, for instance, 46 percent of homeless women reported that they had previously stayed in abusive relationships because they had nowhere to go. In 2003, in Fargo, North Dakota, 44 percent of homeless women reported that they stayed in an abusive relationship at some point in the past two years because they did not have other housing options.

Abusers typically use violence as part of larger strategies to exercise power and control over their partners and isolate their partners from support networks. As a result, a woman who has experienced domestic violence will often have little or no access to money and very few friends or family members to rely on if she flees a violent relationship.

Many landlords have adopted policies, such as "zero tolerance for crime" policies, that penalize victims of domestic violence. These policies allow landlords to evict tenants when violence occurs in their homes, regardless of whether the tenant is the victim or the perpetrator of the violence. A Michigan study of women currently or formerly receiving welfare found that women who had experienced recent or ongoing domestic violence were far more likely to face eviction than other women.

Some landlords are unwilling to rent to a woman who has experienced domestic violence. For example, a 2005 investigation by a fair housing group in New York City found that 28 percent of housing providers either flatly refused to rent to a domestic violence victim or failed to follow up as promised when contacted by an investigator posing as a housing coordinator for a domestic violence survivor assistance program.

Landlords often only learn about domestic violence because victims have sought the help of police or the courts. When victims know that they may face eviction if a landlord finds out about the abuse, they are less likely to seek this assistance and more likely to submit to the abuse.

Domestic Violence and Poverty

Poor women, who are more vulnerable to homelessness, are also at greater risk of domestic violence. Poverty limits women's choices and makes it harder for them to escape violent relationships. . . .

While women at all income levels experience domestic violence, poor women experience domestic violence at higher rates than women with higher household incomes. Women with household incomes of less than $7,500 are 7 times as likely as women with household incomes over $75,000 to experience domestic violence.

Women living in rental housing experience intimate partner violence at three times the rate of women who own their homes.

Homelessness Facts

- In 2005, 50 percent of U.S. cities surveyed reported that domestic violence is a primary cause of homelessness. These cities included Burlington, Cedar Rapids, Charleston, Chicago, Los Angeles, Nashville, Philadelphia, St. Paul, Salt Lake City, San Antonio, Seattle, and Trenton.

- A 2003 survey of homeless mothers around the country found that one quarter had been physically abused in the past year and almost all had experienced or witnessed domestic violence over their lifetimes.

- Forty-seven percent of homeless school-aged children and 29 percent of homeless children under five have witnessed domestic violence in their families, according to a 1999 report.

- A 1997 survey of homeless parents in ten cities around the country found that 22 percent had left their last residence because of domestic violence. Among parents who had lived with a spouse or partner, 57 percent of homeless parents had left their last residence because of domestic violence.

- According to a 1990 study, half of all homeless women and children are fleeing abuse.

American Civil Liberties Union Foundation, 2006.

Women living in poor neighborhoods are more likely to be the victims of domestic violence than women in more affluent neighborhoods. Indeed, women in financially distressed couples who live in poor neighborhoods are twice as likely to be victims of domestic violence than women in equally financially distressed relationships living in more affluent neighborhoods.

Protecting Battered Women's Homes

One way to reduce the risk of homelessness for domestic violence victims is to protect them from housing discrimination on the basis of domestic violence. For this reason. the American Bar Association (ABA) has urged lawmakers to prohibit this form of discrimination. As the report accompanying the ABA's recommendation explained, "Until we stop asking women to choose between being beaten and being able to feed and shelter their children, we cannot expect to rid our society of domestic violence."

In 2005, a federal law was adopted prohibiting many kinds of discrimination against victims of domestic violence who live in public housing or Section 8 housing [in which a subsidy makes up the difference between the contracted rent and the amount a renter is able to pay]. This law states, for instance, that being a victim of domestic violence is not alone a reason for eviction from public housing or loss of a housing voucher. This law, however, does not address discrimination in other kinds of housing against individuals who have experienced domestic violence.

Some states, most notably Washington, Rhode Island, and North Carolina, have adopted broader laws specifically prohibiting housing discrimination against domestic violence victims. Most states, however, either have no laws at all explicitly protecting domestic violence victims' housing rights or have laws that offer only narrow protection in certain circumstances. Some states, for instance, only prohibit evicting those victims of domestic violence who have obtained restraining orders against their abusers. While states are moving in the right direction, these kinds of technicalities limit many state laws' effectiveness in reducing domestic violence and subsequent homelessness.

> *"[American] veterans ... have first-hand experience with homelessness that is a direct consequence of American military and domestic policies."*

American Wars Create Homelessness

Coalition for the Homeless

U.S. military action not only creates homelessness in nations where combat occurs, it also increases the risk of homelessness for American veterans, maintains the Coalition for the Homeless in the following viewpoint. From the Civil War to the Vietnam War, American military policies have created a legion of homeless veterans who suffer from combat-related disabilities, the author asserts. Regrettably, the coalition claims, the U.S. government has failed to provide adequate housing assistance for its low-income or disabled veterans, and without housing assistance for Iraq veterans, a whole new generation of homeless veterans will emerge.

As you read, consider the following questions:

1. According to the Coalition for the Homeless, after what war did "vagrancy" become a nationally recognized issue?

Coalition for the Homeless, "Briefing Paper: War and Homelessness: How American Wars Create Homelessness Among United States Armed Forces Veterans," March 27, 2003. Reproduced by permission.

2. After what war did the link between homelessness and military veterans come to the attention of the general public, in the author's view?

3. In the author's opinion, what would be the immediate and effective way to prevent homelessness among Iraq veterans?

It is axiomatic that wars create homelessness in the territories where combat occurs. Every war that the United States has been involved in, from the Revolutionary War to Desert Storm, has at least temporarily displaced population and destroyed the homes of civilians. Even the "undeclared" wars that the United States has sponsored and supported, in Latin America and elsewhere, produced hundreds of thousands of refugees and uprooted rural and urban populations. However, since the Civil War there have been no sustained military battles fought on United States territory, so most Americans have no first-hand contact with the immediate impact of homelessness resulting from war.

In contrast, our armed forces veterans do have first-hand experience with homelessness that is a direct consequence of American military and domestic policies. This briefing paper provides an overview of the impact of homelessness on armed forces veterans, both historically and currently. Throughout American history there has been high incidence of homelessness among veterans, primarily as a result of combat-related disabilities and trauma and the failure of government benefits to provide adequate housing assistance for low-income and disabled veterans. The paper concludes that, absent a dramatic change in Federal policies, the war on Iraq will create a new generation of homeless veterans.

War and Homeless Veterans in American History

Homelessness in the United States dates back to the colonial era, and rising numbers of "vagabonds" were noted in urban areas in the wake of the Revolutionary War. New York City Mayor Richard Varick noted in 1784 that "Vagrants multiply on our Hands to an amazing Degree," and overcrowding in jails, workhouses, and almshouses led to the construction of a new four-story facility in 1796. However, as noticeable as the rise in homelessness was in the cities and in the Northeast, it was, according to historian Kenneth Kusmer, mitigated in the rural South by the expansion of the system of slave labor.

The post–Civil War era witnessed a much more significant growth in homelessness nationwide. Indeed, as Kusmer notes, "even the words 'tramp' and 'bum,' as applied to the homeless, can be traced to the Civil War era." One reason was the enormous economic dislocation generated by the war and the succeeding economic recession, and by the 1870s "vagrancy" was recognized as a national issue. Many of the new nomads riding the rails and congregating in cities were Civil War veterans, and many had suffered physical injuries and trauma during the war. As the early 1870s recession deepened, many cities responded by creating new anti-vagrancy legislation. In 1874 the number of reported vagrants in Boston was 98,263, more than three times the number just two years earlier. From 1874 to 1878 the number of vagrancy arrests in New York City rose by half.

The homelessness crisis of the Great Depression, which affected many World War I veterans, was dramatically abated in the early 1940s by the enlistment of tens of thousands of Americans in the armed forces and by the wartime economic upswing. In New York City, according to Kusmer, "In one two-month period in 1943, 100 Bowery residents joined the armed forces, while another 200 acquired jobs in hospitals, restaurants, or on the railroads." With the end of World War II, however, homelessness re-emerged as a significant problem in many cities. In New York City, demand for emergency shelter rose in the late 1940s, with as many as 900 men bedding down in the Lodging House Annex (later the Municipal

Period of Active Duty in the Armed Forces for Homeless Veterans	
Period of Active Duty*	
August 1990 or later (Gulf War Era)	8%
September 1980 to July 1990	17%
May 1975 to August 1980	32%
August 1964 to April 1975 (Vietnam Era)	47%
February 1955 to July 1964	15%
June 1950 to January 1955 (Korean conflict)	4%
September 1940 to July 1947 (World War II)	1%
Any other time	1%

*Total does not equal 100%, since some individuals served in more than one period of active duty.

TAKEN FROM: Urban Institute, *National Survey of Homeless Assistance Providers and Clients* (1999).

Shelter) on East 3rd Street in the 1948–49 winter. Homelessness would have continued to affect many thousands of World War II veterans were it not for the national economic upturn and the benefits provided by the G.I. Bill.

A New Wave of Homeless Persons

With the advent of the Vietnam War, however, the link between homelessness and military veterans finally came to the attention of the general public. As Kusmer writes, "Only a few years after the end of the war . . . a new wave of homeless persons, mostly in their 20s and 30s and disproportionately black or Hispanic, began to appear on city street corners. Many were Vietnam veterans, unable to find work after being discharged." By the late 1970s, when modern homelessness fully emerged, a significant portion of the homeless men seen sleeping outdoors in vast numbers in New York City and other large cities were armed forces veterans. Many veterans suffered from post traumatic stress disorder (PTSD), substance abuse disorders, and physical disabilities caused by their experiences in combat.

The 1991 Gulf War, the last major conventional war involving the United States military, also left many veterans recovering from physical and mental disabilities and confronting homelessness. A 1997 survey of 1,200 homeless veterans nationwide who resided at mission shelters found that 10 percent of them were Gulf War veterans. In New York City, homeless service providers also reported assisting significant numbers of Desert Storm veterans.

The Current Status of Homeless Veterans

The United States Department of Veterans Affairs (VA) estimates that on a given night some 250,000 veterans are homeless nationwide, and that as many as half a million veterans experience homeless[ness] in the course of a year; this represents around two percent of all living American veterans. All but 3 percent of homeless veterans are men, and 56 percent are black or Latino. Approximately 45 percent suffer from mental illness, and more than two-thirds suffer from substance abuse disorders. More than two-thirds of homeless veterans served in the armed forces for at least three years, and 47 percent served in the Vietnam War.

According to a 1996 nationwide survey of homeless people and service providers, 33 percent of the male homeless population is comprised of veterans, and 23 percent of the total homeless population is made up of veterans. In New York City, nearly one of every ten municipal shelter beds for homeless single men is set aside for homeless veterans, and annually thousands of homeless veterans utilize municipal and private shelters or reside in public spaces.

The principal cause of homelessness among veterans is the failure of VA disability benefits and other public benefits to provide adequate and appropriate housing assistance. According to the National Coalition for Homeless Veterans, the VA's homeless programs assist only 40,000 veterans each year, less than 10 percent of the estimated number of veterans who experience homelessness annually. Given the high prevalence of mental illness and other disabilities among homeless veterans, the need for supportive housing (i.e., housing with on-site support services for individuals living with mental illness and other disabilities) and affordable housing assistance is critical. Nevertheless, VA benefits and other public benefits are not adequate to allow most veterans—particularly those in urban areas like New York City—to afford rental housing, and the supply of supportive housing nationally for disabled homeless individuals is woefully inadequate.

A New Generation of Homeless Veterans

Without a dramatic change in Federal policies—including substantial increases in housing assistance and supportive housing investments for homeless and at-risk veterans—there is no doubt that the war on Iraq will create a new generation of homeless veterans. More than 200,000 members of the United States armed forces are currently stationed in the Persian Gulf, and many more may potentially serve in the area in the likely event of a prolonged United States occupation of the region.

There are a number of steps the Federal government and the Congress could take to prevent homelessness among veterans. These would include:

- *Mandating adequate housing assistance as part of the package of veterans benefits.* This could be accomplished by augmenting existing VA benefits or by establishing an entitlement to rental housing vouchers for income-eligible veterans.

- *Providing an adequate supply of supportive housing for homeless veterans.* This could be accomplished by expanding funding for existing VA and Department

of Housing and Urban Development (HUD) supportive housing programs. . . .

There is no indication that changes in Federal policies
necessary to prevent a new wave of homelessness among
American veterans are even a remote possibility. Indeed, it is
much more likely that the . . . direction of [the George W.]
Bush Administration budget policies will contribute to increased homelessness among veterans as well as low-income
families and individuals.

Of course, the most immediate and effective way to prevent homelessness among a new generation of armed forces
veterans would be to bring the troops currently stationed in
Iraq and the Persian Gulf back home. Finally, it is essential to
recall that the war effort will displace countless Iraqis and de-
stroy an untold number of Iraqi homes. Aside from the political challenges that will confront post-war Iraq, the rebuilding
effort must address the housing needs (as well as the nutri-
tional and health care needs) of the Iraqi population and of
refugees to avert a wave of homelessness in the Persian Gulf
region.

"The 'working homeless'—a post-welfare-reform category of strivers [are] fighting to hold onto low-wage jobs . . . that perversely afford them too little money to pay for shelter."

Welfare Reform Increases Homelessness

Francis X. Clines

In the following viewpoint Francis X. Clines argues that welfare reform has created a new category of American—the working homeless. For example, homeless working mothers, Clines claims, now commute long distances from homeless shelters just to keep their low-paying food-service jobs. Welfare reform may have put people to work, he asserts, but these low-wage jobs do not leave workers with enough money to pay for housing. In fact, he points out, homelessness is increasing nationwide. Clines writes on national political issues for the New York Times.

As you read, consider the following questions:

1. In Clines's opinion, what population makes up the majority of working homeless that social workers are tracking?

2. What problem does Clines claim has grown steadily, despite the economic boom of the 1990s?

3. What hourly wage would be required to pay for a two-bedroom family rental in St. Louis, in the author's view?

The jargon of antipoverty work is as restless as the poor themselves. And here now come the "working homeless"—a post-welfare-reform category of strivers fighting to hold onto low-wage jobs the government shepherded them to, jobs that perversely afford them too little money to pay for shelter. Ending welfare as we know it has been followed by the working homeless, if we care to know them.

Marginal Breadwinners

Social workers are tracking these marginal breadwinners by the scores of thousands—most of them women with children, not the stereotypical grizzled street male. They can be found here spiraling through desperate options when they come up short for rent money and are displaced. Many serially "couch surf" with relatives and friends before patience wears thin. Some live as families in a car or a spare garage space. Chronically, they turn to the waiting lists for transient shelters that are always filled to capacity in this hard-pressed but far from atypical American city.

Citizens who hailed the statistical success of welfare reform in thinning down the dole need to see the hard aftermath in which the new workfare is producing a variation on some old misery for the working homeless. "They've traded one form of poverty for another," says Katrina Knight, the director of the Housing Resource Center. The center runs the hotline in St. Louis, [Missouri,] which leads the nation's major cities in their common problem of facing the highest increase in demands for emergency shelter and food in a decade.

The darkening economy is compounding a homeless problem that, despite the 90's boom, grew steadily, near-

Increasing the Risk of Homelessness

Slashed public assistance has also left many people homeless or at risk of homelessness. Replacement of the Aid to Families with Dependent Children (AFDC) entitlement program—a program that was already inadequate in meeting the needs of families—with the non-entitlement block grant program will significantly increase the risk of homelessness for many Americans. According to the House Ways and Means Committee, AFDC represents less than half of the poverty threshold in three out of four states. Furthermore, earned income and asset limitations discourage individuals and families from breaking the cycle of homelessness and extreme poverty.

National Law Center on Homelessness & Poverty, 2002.

subliminally, across the prosperity era. The U.S. Conference of Mayors, which has been annually surveying homelessness and hunger in 25 major cities since 1987, warns that we're ending a bumper year [2002] for the problem. Cities registered a one-year increase of 19 percent in food and shelter requests—with another tough year looming as tax revenues fall and political priorities shift to homeland security.

Struggling with Low Wages and Joblessness

The St. Louis increase was more than double the urban average and may be due to better records in tracking the ricochet world of the homeless. But it is the nature of the increased pleas even more than the volume that is stark for workers at the Salvation Army's Community in Partnership family shelter at the edge of the city. [Since 2000] they have seen a doubling of homeless applicants still scrabbling to maintain jobs. In fact, four of five requests at the shelter now come from families led by a dogged wage earner, albeit a marginal one. Mothers commute long hours from the shelter to hold onto fast-food service jobs. Their problem is that, by local average, it requires a wage of $12 an hour to pay for the two-bedroom family rental they yearn for and earn for, but their actual wage is little more than the $5.15 government minimum.

At the hotline, workers can be heard taking more calls from people who begin by noting they [have] never asked for charity in their lives but are facing mortgage foreclosure in a middle-class neighborhood amid a grueling struggle with joblessness. "I never imagined I'd be here," said Richard, a jobless stage-set designer, sitting forlornly at a holiday party of the homeless from the Peter & Paul shelter. "This is humiliating," he said, ruing his predicament as a working homeless person whose current threadbare livelihood is in a sandwich shop. "It's unbelievable how fast you can lose the good life."

More poignant are the tales of working homeless mothers who never tasted the middle-class heights. With hopes high, they spend off-hours in a bureaucratic maze in order to finally win one of the federal rent subsidy vouchers. These vouchers are widely coveted as a key opportunity upward by many of the nation's millions of working poor who are without housing assistance. Jeanette, a woman with three children, turned suicidal after she scoured the city for an apartment for three months and discovered that landlords dismissed her hard-won voucher as worthless in their tight renters' market. "She thought she had won a lottery," said Ms. Knight. "She's left much more dejected and fragile."

Worse news is on the way to the nation's mayors and their homeless. The rent voucher program, designed to have the poor pay no more than 30 percent of income for shelter, is already being targeted in Congress. A bill favored by the Appropriations Committee in the Republican-controlled House would cut more than $900 million from President Bush's plan for voucher aid, according to advocates for the poor. [The

2003 budget renewed only those section 8 vouchers currently in use.] They estimate 125,000 families would lose vouchers in a program that serves about two million poor and dates honorably from the [Richard] Nixon and [Ronald] Reagan eras.

Periodical Bibliography

The following articles have been selected to supplement the diverse views presented in this chapter.

Laverne Ballard — "God Bless the Child: A Woman Who Grew Up Sleeping in the Streets Tells Her Haunting Story," *Essence*, September 2006.

Colby Berger — "What Becomes of At-Risk Gay Youths?" *The Gay & Lesbian Review Worldwide*, November/December 2005.

Thomas H. Bornemann — "Mental Health System Needs a Life," *Washington Post*, May 29, 2004.

Carol L. M. Caton et al. — "Risk Factors for Long-Term Homelessness," *American Journal of Public Health*, October 2005.

Chicago Coalition for the Homeless — "Homelessness: The Causes and the Facts," *The Facts Behind the Faces*, Winter 2004–2005.

Les Gapay — "How a Regular Guy Gets Homeless," *USA Today*, September 22, 2003.

Martin Gittelman — "The Neglected Disaster," *International Journal of Mental Health*, June 2005.

Phillip Hozer — "Get a Job!' Eight Myths and Misconceptions About People Who Are Homeless," *Cross Currents: The Journal of Addiction and Mental Health*, Summer 2006.

Maurice Martin — "Living Wage Offers Ray of Light for Homeless," *People's Weekly World*, May 19, 2005.

Suzanne Speak — "Relationship Between Children's Homelessness in Developing Countries and the Failure of Women's Rights Legislation," *Housing, Theory and Society*, 2005.

Kevin J. Swick — "The Dynamics of Families Who Are Homeless," *Childhood Education*, Spring 2004.

CHAPTER 3

What Housing Policies Will Benefit the Homeless?

Chapter Preface

One of several controversies in the housing policy debate is whether housing-first programs are the best way to reduce homelessness. For those who believe that a lack of affordable housing and poverty are responsible for homelessness, programs that provide permanent, affordable housing are best. Other commentators claim, however, that homelessness is not simply a housing problem but the result of a more complex set of concerns. In addition to providing immediate housing needs, these analysts argue, the existing shelter system could provide on-site services and programs that address the complex causes of homelessness.

Those who advocate housing-first programs argue that a lack of affordable housing is the root cause of homelessness. According to Beyond Shelter, "While it is often the result of interwoven systemic and personal problems, the primary cause of homelessness among families is the growing gap between housing costs and income." Unfortunately, Beyond Shelter argues, the traditional approach to the problem of homelessness, the emergency shelter system, has failed "to provide the intensive long-term assistance that homeless families require in order to stabilize their lives." While shelters meet immediate housing needs, Beyond Shelter claims, "they often fail to address the long-term needs of homeless families. Families need help in finding affordable housing, negotiating leases and developing the skills to stay housed." According to the National Alliance to End Homelessness, housing-first programs "place families as quickly as possible in permanent housing, and then provide intensive home-based case management and stabilizing support services to prevent a recurrence of homelessness." Shelter programs, the alliance claims, are designed to help people become ready for housing. The first priority of housing-first programs, the alliance maintains, is to help the homeless get housed immediately. "By helping participants become housed and connected to mainstream services," the alliance argues, "Housing First programs can help prevent them from entering or help them rapidly exit the homeless service system."

Some activists claim, however, that while housing is an admirable goal, the reality is that "homelessness is not simply a housing issue. Rather, it stems from poor education, lack of employable skills, inadequate health care, domestic violence, child abuse, foster care, and insufficient child care," assert Ralph da Costa Nuñez and Laura M. Caruso of Homes for the Homeless. "Many of today's homeless families are headed by a young unmarried mother, with two or three children," da Costa Nuñez and Caruso claim. "She grew up in poverty, may have experienced domestic violence, and never completed high school, often dropping out due to pregnancy. She has at least one child suffering from a chronic health problem and has had trouble enrolling her kids in school," they maintain. Having few options, these homeless families turn to shelters to keep their families together. "It is here—in shelters—that the reduction of family homelessness may actually begin," da Costa Nuñez and Caruso argue. "Shelters and transitional housing themselves may be the catalyst for reducing homelessness by providing on-site services and programs that address the root causes of this new poverty," they reason. According to da Costa Nuñez and Caruso, the national shelter infrastructure already in place can be used to provide enhanced services that focus on "building long-term skills that foster independence and economic viability. If we take the emergency out of the situation and allow them to focus on building real skills and work histories, we offer families their first step on a path to self-determination."

Commentators continue to contest whether shelters with enhanced services or housing-first policies are the best way to help the homeless. The authors in the following chapter debate other issues in the housing policy controversy.

> *"Is there really a human right to housing? The answer is emphatically yes."*

Housing Is a Human Right

René Heybach and Patricia Nix-Hodes

International law recognizes adequate housing as a human right, claims René Heybach and Patricia Nix-Hodes in the following viewpoint. In 1948, for example, the United Nations recognized a right to housing in the Universal Declaration of Human Rights, the authors assert. When the United States cuts housing subsidies to reduce corporate taxes, the authors argue, it violates these laws. Heybach is director of the Law Project, and Nix-Hodes is senior staff attorney for the Chicago Coalition for the Homeless, a nationally recognized housing advocacy organization.

As you read, consider the following questions:

1. To what covenants is the United States a party to and/or signatory of, according to Heybach and Nix-Hodes?
2. In the authors' view, what are some of the components of "adequate housing"?
3. In Heybach and Nix-Hodes' opinion, what does it mean when a government tolerates the deprivation of basic shelter and housing?

René Heybach and Patricia Nix-Hodes, "Chicago Coaltion for the Homeless Policy Paper: Is Housing a Human Right?" *Homeward Bound*, Fall 2003. Reproduced by permission.

Since its inception, the Chicago Coalition for the Homeless has asserted its belief that "housing is a human right in a just society." But is there really a human right to housing? The answer is emphatically yes. The right to adequate housing is recognized as a basic and fundamental human right in many sources of international human rights law.

Where Is the Right to Housing Found?

The right to housing was initially recognized as part of the right to an adequate standard of living, as enunciated in the Universal Declaration of Human Rights, adopted by the United Nations in 1948. All member states of the United Nations are bound to respect and observe the rights contained in the Universal Declaration, which states in part:

> Everyone has the right to a standard of living adequate for the health and well-being of himself [or herself] and of his [or her] family, including food, clothing, *housing* and medical care, and necessary social services, and the right to security in the event of unemployment, sickness, disability, widowhood or other lack of livelihood in circumstances beyond his [or her] control. [Emphasis supplied.]

The right to adequate housing is contained in many other international human rights instruments, including, principally, the International Covenant on Economic, Social and Cultural Rights (ICESCR), which necognizes:

> [T]he right of everyone to an adequate standard of living for himself [or herself] and his [or her family, including adequate food, clothing *and housing*, and to the continuous improvement of living conditions. [Emphasis supplied.]

Housing rights language also is contained in Article 17 of the International Covenant on Civil and Political Rights, which protects persons from arbitrary or unlawful interference with their home; Article 5(e)(iii) of the International Convention on the Elimination of All Forms of Racial Discrimination,

111

which prohibits discrimination in the right to housing; Article 14(2)(H) of the Convention on the Elimination of All Forms of Discrimination against Women, which prohibits discrimination against women, in part to ensure that women enjoy adequate housing; Article 27(3) of the Convention on the Rights of the Child; and many other sources.

While the United States is not a party to all these instruments, it is a party to the International Covenant on Civil and Political Rights, and the International Convention on the Elimination of All Forms of Racial Discrimination. With respect to the International Covenant on Economic, Social and Cultural Rights, which contains the strongest and most specific right-to-housing language, the United States has signed but not yet ratified the Covenant. As a signatory, however, the United States cannot defeat the object or purpose of the Covenant, for example by adopting "retrogressive" measures with respect to the economic, social, and cultural rights contained within the Covenant. Such measures could include, for example, cutting existing critical housing subsidies to provide tax cuts to corporations or repealing legislation that accorded some form of housing rights. Moreover, the right to housing arguably has evolved into "customary international law" to which the United States and other countries are bound even if the countries have not ratified the ICESCR.

What Are the Elements of the Right to Housing?

The United Nations Committee on Economic, Social and Cultural Rights unanimously adopted General Comment No. 4 on the Right to Adequate Housing in 1991. At that time, the Committee noted the United Nations' estimate of over 100 million homeless persons worldwide. Recent estimates note that more than 2 billion people are inadequately housed.

The General Comment is the most authoritative legal interpretation of what the right to housing actually means. Gen-

A Universal Right

The right to housing is a human right which extends to EVERYONE: men, women and children. This right must not be subject to any form of discrimination and should be ensured to all persons irrespective of income or access to economic resources.

Center for Economic and Social Rights, http://cesr.org.

eral Comment No. 4 states that the right to housing "should not be interpreted in a narrow or restrictive sense which equates it with, for example, the shelter provided by merely having a roof over one's head," but rather should be viewed as the right to live in "security, peace and dignity." Importantly, the General Comment recognizes that the right to housing should be available to all people "irrespective of income or access to economic resources." Further, the Committee recognized that the concept of "adequacy" of housing is crucial to the right to housing and identified a number of components of "adequate housing," including:

- *Legal security of tenure*—"[A]ll persons should possess a degree of security of tenure which guarantees legal protection against forced eviction, harassment and other threats;"

- *Availability of service, materials, facilities and infrastructure*—"[A]n adequate house must contain certain facilities essential for health, security, comfort and nutrition;"

- *Affordability*—Housing costs should not be so high as to compromise the satisfaction of other basic needs;

- *Habitability*—Housing should include adequate space and protection from cold, damp, heat, rain, wind or other threats to health;

- *Accessibility*—Housing should take into account the special needs of groups such as the elderly, children, the physically disabled, the terminally ill, HIV-positive individuals, the mentally ill and other groups;
- *Location*—Housing must be in a location accessible to employment, healthcare, school, childcare and other social services;
- *Cultural adequacy*—Expression of cultural identity and diversity in housing must be enabled.

What Are the Implications of the Right to Housing in the United States?

The full meaning and content of the right to adequate housing as applied to the United States is complex and simply beyond the scope of this brief article. Suffice it to say these rights do not generally oblige governments immediately to build housing for everyone but rather imply an obligation to move expeditiously toward that objective. In particular, however, obligations are more pressing with respect to homeless persons and to government-endorsed actions that result in homelessness.

Significantly, according to the Committee on Economic, Social and Cultural Rights, for a government to tolerate the deprivation of basic shelter and housing for a significant number of its people is a *prima facie* violation of the obligations of the Covenant. Such lack of housing compels some immediate action to address the need. In addition, the right to adequate housing guarantees protection against "forced eviction." Government-sponsored, planned efforts to displace significant numbers of people from their homes resulting in homelessness clearly implicate the prohibition of forced eviction. The "transformation" of public housing ... in the United States has displaced thousands of persons against their will and rendered many persons homeless while triggering international concern for the human rights of these former public housing residents.

"*[The solution to homelessness] is a debate that is not advanced by defining housing as a human right.*"

Housing Is Not a Human Right

Michael Tanner

According to Michael Tanner in the following viewpoint, affordable housing is not a human right. A properly defined right should not conflict with other rights, he argues. A right to housing, however, does interfere with the rights of others. It may deprive some of money in the form of tax dollars and others of the right to determine the rent they may charge, he maintains. Tanner is director of health and welfare studies at the Cato Institute, a libertarian think tank in Washington, D.C.

As you read, consider the following questions:

1. How does Tanner explain the negative character of properly defined rights?
2. In the author's opinion, how far could the positive obligations of a right to housing go?
3. From what do a majority of homeless suffer, in Tanner's view?

A ffordable housing for every American is a desirable goal for public policy. But not every good policy can be translated into questions of human rights.

The Nature of Rights

When properly defined, rights do not conflict. That is because rights are essentially negatives in character. My exercise of my rights in no way infringes on your exercise of your rights. Your only obligation is negative, to refrain from interfering with my exercise of rights. Thus, my right to speak freely requires no action on your part, takes nothing away from you. My right exists independent of you. Your only obligation is not to stop me from speaking.

But the same is not true of a right to affordable housing. It would impose a positive obligation. In order for me to exercise my right, something must be taken away from you. That may be your property, directly through taxes, or indirectly through limits on what you can charge for rent. But in theory, my claim on you could go still further. Suppose there simply was not enough housing being built. If housing is a right, I would have the authority to conscript you to become a carpenter.

This can be expanded even further. Rights are universal, not subject to national borders. Therefore, if housing is a right, people's property and liberty would be subject to appropriation not just to solve homelessness in this country, but until every person worldwide had housing.

And, of course, one shudders at the definitional question. What qualifies as housing sufficient to satisfy the right? A mud hut, a single room, a ranch-style bungalow?

Beyond the philosophical, there are practical questions involved. Simply declaring something a "right" does nothing to actually solve the problems leading to homelessness. Homelessness is not simply a question of lack of money or lack of inexpensive housing. The majority of homeless suffer from

mental illness and/or drug and alcohol problems. If given a house or apartment today, many would be homeless again tomorrow.

The problems underlying homelessness are complex and the solutions subject to considerable debate. That is a debate worth having, but it is a debate that is not advanced by defining housing as a human right.

> *"Vouchers have generally allowed assisted families to disperse more widely and to live in lower-poverty, less-segregated neighborhoods."*

Housing Vouchers Benefit Low-Income Families

Margery Austin Turner

In the following viewpoint Margery Austin Turner maintains that housing vouchers, a housing assistance program that supplements the rent payments of low-income families, allow these families to live in better neighborhoods. Participants in housing-choice programs hold higher-income jobs, and their children do better in school, Turner asserts. To cut voucher program funding would restrict the mobility of low-income families, trapping them in a cycle of poverty. Turner is director of the Metropolitan Housing and Communities Policy Center at the Urban Institute, an economic and social policy think tank.

As you read, consider the following questions:

1. In Turner's view, how are housing vouchers different from previous low-income housing programs?

Margery Austin Turner, "Preserving the Strengths of the Housing Choice Voucher Program," Statement before the Subcommittee on Housing and Community Opportunity, Committee on Financial Services, United States House of Representatives, May 17, 2005. Reproduced by permission.

2. According to the author, in what ways does living in a distressed, high-poverty neighborhood undermine the well-being of families?

3. What are some of the benefits of escaping from distressed neighborhoods to healthier communities, in Turner's opinion?

The Housing Choice Voucher program plays a critical role in our nation's housing policy.... Vouchers supplement rent payments for 1.7 million low-income families and individuals, making it the nation's largest housing assistance program. Recipients choose a house or apartment available in the private market and contribute about 30 percent of their incomes toward rent, while the federal government pays the difference—up to a locally defined "payment standard." Families with vouchers can move to any jurisdiction that administers a voucher program. Compared with unassisted households at comparable income levels, voucher recipients are far less likely to be paying unaffordable housing cost burdens and more likely to be living in decent quality housing. And because the voucher program relies on the existing housing stock, it is less costly than programs that build new projects for occupancy by the poor.

The Benefits of Vouchers

One of the greatest strengths of the voucher program is that it allows families to choose the type of housing and neighborhood that best meets their needs. Historically, many low-income housing programs have exacerbated the geographic concentration of poor families, especially minorities, in high-poverty neighborhoods. For example, 37 percent of public housing residents live in neighborhoods where the poverty rate exceeds 40 percent, and most African American residents of public housing live in neighborhoods that are majority black. Even more recent housing production programs, such as the Low Income Housing Tax Credit [LIHTC] and the HOME program, have placed a disproportionate share of assisted units in poor and minority neighborhoods. For example, almost half of LIHTC units are located in neighborhoods that are predominantly black.

In contrast, vouchers have generally allowed assisted families to disperse more widely and to live in lower-poverty, less-segregated neighborhoods. In fact, the latest research finds at least some voucher recipients living in 8 out of 10 neighborhoods in large metropolitan areas. Specifically, [Deborah J.] Devine [and Robert W. Gray, Lester Rubin, and Lydia B. Taghaui] analyze the spatial distribution of voucher recipients in the nation's 50 largest metropolitan areas and conclude that nearly every census tract in these areas contains some housing at rent levels accessible to voucher recipients; voucher recipients are currently living in 83 percent of these census tracts. As a consequence, 59 percent of voucher recipients live in neighborhoods that are less than 20 percent poor, and only 22 percent live in neighborhoods with poverty rates in excess of 30 percent.

Why Choice Matters

Social science research clearly shows that living in a distressed, high-poverty neighborhood undermines the well-being of families and the long-term life chances of children. There is ample evidence that residents of poor, inner-city neighborhoods are less likely to complete high school and go on to college, more likely to be involved in crime (either as victims or as perpetrators), more likely to be teenage parents, and less likely to hold decent-paying jobs. Actually quantifying the independent effect of neighborhood conditions on outcomes for individual residents is more challenging. But in general, well-designed empirical research that controls statistically for individual and family attributes finds that neighborhood environment has a significant influence on important life outcomes for both children and adults.

Infants and Young Children. Several studies have found that having more affluent neighbors is associated with higher IQ for preschool children, and elementary school performance is linked to neighborhood social and economic status.

Adolescents. Young people from high-poverty and distressed neighborhoods are less successful in school than their counterparts from more affluent communities; they earn lower grades, are more likely to drop out, and are less likely to go on to college. Studies have also documented that neighborhood environment influences teens' sexual activity and the likelihood that girls will become pregnant during their teen years. And finally, young people who live in high-crime areas have been found to be more likely to commit crimes themselves.

Adults. Considerable research has found evidence that distance from jobs reduces employment rates, particularly among lower-skilled adults. Additionally, research suggests that living in disadvantaged neighborhoods increases the risk of mortality and disease, other things being equal.

Improving Lives

When families are able to escape from distressed neighborhoods and move to healthier communities, their lives improve measurably. Research on families who have moved through the Gautreaux demonstration, the Moving to Opportunity (MTO) demonstration, and the HOPE VI program provides evidence of significant benefits for both parents and children.[1]

- *Greater Safety and Security.* Research on participants in the Moving to Opportunity (MTO) demonstration finds that moving to low-poverty neighbor-

1. The Gautreaux demonstration provided special-purpose vouchers and counseling to African American families who moved from poor, predominantly black neighborhoods in Chicago to racially integrated communities in the city and its suburbs. The MTO demonstration is a carefully controlled experiment to test the impacts of helping families move from high-poverty assisted housing projects to low-poverty neighborhoods.

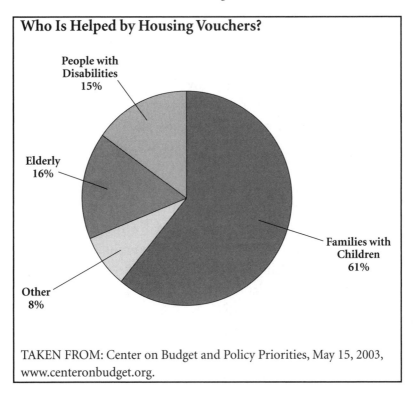

Who Is Helped by Housing Vouchers?

People with Disabilities 15%

Elderly 16%

Other 8%

Families with Children 61%

TAKEN FROM: Center on Budget and Policy Priorities, May 15, 2003, www.centeronbudget.org.

hoods produced a 30 percentage point increase in perceptions of safety. We see similar gains among HOPE VI relocatees. From the perspective of families, this means moving from a gang- and drug-infested neighborhood where shooting is the norm to a neighborhood where children can go outside to play.

- *Better Schools.* Gautreaux research found striking benefits for children whose families moved to suburban neighborhoods. They were substantially more likely to complete high school, take college-track courses, attend college, and enter the workforce than children from similar families who moved to neighborhoods within Chicago. MTO families have moved to neighborhoods with better schools, but—unlike

Gautreaux movers—relatively few have left central-city school districts. Moreover, some MTO children continue to attend the same schools, despite the fact that their families have moved. So far, there is no evidence that MTO moves have led to better educational outcomes, possibly because so few children are attending significantly better schools or because it may be too soon to see benefits. HOPE VI relocatees who have moved with vouchers report improvements in the schools their children attend. They see the schools as safer and [of] better quality, and they also report that their kids are having fewer problems at school, including trouble with teachers, disobedience at school and at home, and problems getting along with other children.

- *Better Outcomes for Teenage Girls.* Some of the early research on MTO families in individual sites suggested that young people whose families moved to low-poverty neighborhoods were engaging in less risky behavior and committing fewer crimes. More recent and comprehensive data for all sites suggest that moving to a lower-poverty environment is indeed improving the behavior of teen-age girls, but not boys.

- *Improved Health.* The MTO demonstration has shown dramatic improvements in the health of the families who moved to lower-poverty neighborhoods. In particular, the most recent evidence shows a substantial reduction in adult obesity. MTO and adolescent girls also showed significant improvements in mental health, including reductions in psychological distress and depression.

- *Employment and Earnings.* Long-term research on Gautreaux families has found significant increases in employment and reductions in welfare receipt. To date, no statistically significant employment or earnings gains have been found across the total sample of MTO families or among HOPE VI relocatees. However, analysis of individual MTO sites finds significant gains in employment and earnings among MTO families in New York and Los Angeles, and exploratory analysis suggests that families who moved to the healthiest neighborhoods have experienced significant increases in earnings.

The Administration Proposal Would Limit Choice

The proposed State and Local Housing Flexibility Act of 2005 takes the voucher program in the wrong direction. The bill threatens to severely restrict mobility and housing choice. Specifically, families would not be permitted to use their housing vouchers to move from one jurisdiction to another unless the administering housing agencies had a standing agreement. In other words, suburban jurisdictions could simply refuse to accept voucher holders seeking to move out of distressed city neighborhoods in order to be closer to job opportunities or to give their children the advantages of attending safe, high-performing public schools.

Moves within a jurisdiction—for example, from higher-poverty neighborhoods to lower-poverty neighborhoods within a city or town—could be restricted as well. The proposed bill allows [public] housing agencies [PHAs] to set payment standards (which determine subsidy levels) without considering data on actual rent levels. Already facing severe funding constraints, housing agencies may feel pressured to set their payment standards lower in order to serve more families. But ultimately, lower payment standards will make vouchers less competitive in the rental market and could severely limit neighborhood choice. Moreover, "exception rents," a provision that allows for higher payment standards in high-cost areas, would likely be discontinued under the Administration's proposal. In effect, local housing agencies would be left to choose between serving more families in higher-poverty neighborhoods or fewer families in opportunity-rich neighborhoods. Finally, the performance measurement system HUD [U.S. Department of Housing and Urban Development] currently uses to monitor housing agency success in helping families move to better neighborhoods is likely to be discontinued and replaced by new (not yet specified) performance indicators for assessing the performance of local voucher programs. This will eliminate existing incentives for PHAs to help families move to neighborhoods of choice and opportunity.

Creating Hardship and Insecurity

The Administration's proposal also creates strong financial pressures on local housing agencies to use scarce voucher resources to serve more families at higher-income levels, rather than targeting assistance to extremely low-income families, who require deeper subsidies in order to pay for housing in the private market. Because vouchers have the advantage of dispersing assisted families geographically (rather than clustering them in subsidized developments), they provide a particularly valuable tool for addressing the severe housing needs of the lowest income levels. In other words, project-based housing subsidy resources need to be spread across a wider range of income levels in order to create healthy, mixed-income communities, but vouchers can promote income mixing even when they are targeted to the lowest income levels. Ideally, housing subsidies of all types would be available for low- and moderate-income families, but in an era of increasingly scarce resources, shifting vouchers away from the most needy families will only exacerbate housing hardship and distress.

Targeting assistance to very-low-income families yields benefits that go beyond housing per se, contributing to the larger policy goals of work and self-sufficiency. Specifically, families with unaffordable housing cost burdens are financially insecure, vulnerable to unexpected increases in other costs, and more likely to have to move frequently. This insecurity can make it more difficult for them to get and keep jobs, work extra hours, or advance to higher wages. In addition, the extra income freed up by a housing subsidy may enable families to pay for reliable child care, transportation to a better job, additional training, or professional clothing—all investments that can enhance employment success. In fact, several recent studies have found that people who receive housing assistance are more likely to benefit from workforce or welfare-to-work programs than people without assistance, after controlling for other household differences.

Finally, the Administration's proposal would allow local housing agencies to experiment with alternative subsidy formulas and even impose time limits on housing assistance. Some have argued that the current subsidy formula (in which families pay about 30 percent of their income toward rent and the voucher makes up the difference) discourages work, because earning more income automatically results in increased rent payments. HUD's Moving to Work demonstration includes several housing agencies that are experimenting with variations in voucher program rules, including fixed subsidy levels, minimum tenant contributions, and time limits. However, the impacts of these alternative approaches are not being rigorously evaluated, because Moving to Work was not designed for this purpose. Therefore, there is no firm evidence to guide local housing agencies in designing new formulas that encourage work without sacrificing access to affordable housing in safe and opportunity-rich neighborhoods. . . .

The Risks of Eliminating Choice

Eliminating the features that promote "choice" in the Housing Choice Voucher program undermines the inherent power of this vital policy tool. Housing and neighborhood choice under

127

the voucher program offer families the chance to move to neighborhoods that meet their needs—relocating to be closer to a new job or to find an apartment in a community with high-performing schools. These opportunities can help families break the cycle of poverty, enhancing their safety and health and providing access to better schools and well-paying job opportunities. . . .

The Administration's proposal actually discourages local housing authorities from implementing . . . proven strategies, and instead creates incentives for cost-cutting measures that would shift assistance away from families with the greatest needs and reduce the purchasing power of a housing voucher. And allowing individual PHAs to implement their own payment standards and subsidy formulas is likely to result in a patchwork of program rules and procedures that could undermine landlords' willingness to participate. The State and Local Housing Flexibility Act of 2005 would move federal housing policy in the wrong direction, trapping families in neighborhoods that are poor and distressed and perpetuating concentrated poverty and isolation from economic opportunities.[2]

2. As of November 2006, the bill remains in committee.

| *"Just like the old welfare system, housing vouchers promote dependency and subsidize irresponsibility."*

Housing Vouchers Do Not Benefit Low-Income Families

Howard Husock

Housing vouchers, a housing assistance program that supplements rent payments, does not help low-income families; it creates a cycle of dependency, argues Howard Husock in the following viewpoint. Housing vouchers are sought primarily by single-parent households who flood homeless shelters because the program gives priority to shelter families, Husock maintains. Income limits give voucher tenants, who are often disruptive and destructive, little motivation to improve their economic situation. Husock is director of case studies in public policy and management at the Kennedy School of Government at Harvard University.

As you read, consider the following questions:

1. According to Husock, what is the median rent that voucher tenants pay in New York City?

Howard Husock, "The Housing Reform That Backfired," *City Journal*, summer 2004. Copyright The Manhattan Institute. Reproduced by permission.

2. How is the meaning of the term "homeless" determined in New York City, in the author's opinion?

3. In Husock's view, what is the false assumption behind all subsidized housing?

Far from protecting "our most vulnerable residents," as Senator [Hillary] Clinton puts it, housing vouchers are a last redoubt of the Democrat-sponsored entitlement culture that wreaked such harm on the poor and vulnerable over the last four decades by making them perpetually dependent.

Housing vouchers—in New York and across urban America—originated [in the early 1970s], with "Section 8" of the Nixon-era National Housing Act. The program's rationale was straightforward: instead of placing an aid recipient in a housing project—viewed as a failed experiment because of the projects' expense and disorder—the federal government would provide a voucher that subsidized the rent in a privately owned apartment. Conservatives have supported the voucher plan over the years chiefly because of its seeming free-market component, and because it does not impose on the government the considerable cost of building and maintaining public housing. But whatever Republican hopes, the voucher initiative operated from its inception just like any other no-strings-attached welfare program—and it continues to do so today, . . . years after the nation ended the federal welfare entitlement and lifted hundreds of thousands of formerly dependent welfare mothers into lives of work and greater personal responsibility.

A Hefty, Open-Ended Benefit

Almost alone among post-welfare reform social programs, Section 8 remains an open-ended benefit, with no time limit. And the benefit it provides is hefty. The median rent that voucher tenants pay in New York, for example, works out to just $220 a month, and many voucher recipients pay $100 or less. The New York City Housing Authority (NYCHA), at federal taxpayers' expense, pays a landlord the remainder of the going rate of $1,180 for a two-bedroom unit and $1,476 for a three-bedroom (utilities included) that the Department of Housing and Urban Development (HUD) approves for the city. Since the law requires that 75 percent of housing vouchers must go to households earning less than 30 percent of an area's median income, the entitlement overwhelmingly supports single-parent households, America's poorest. In other words, housing vouchers abet, just as pre-reform welfare did, the formation and continuation of such households—those most at risk of remaining in long-term poverty and of raising children who end up in the underclass.

That Section 8 is today's face of dependency is most apparent in New York, home to far more voucher holders than any other U.S. city. Even as Gotham's welfare rolls shrank dramatically after welfare reform, the city's housing voucher program ballooned. NYCHA's allotment of vouchers has risen 21 percent, from 74,000 to 90,000, [from 2000–2004] alone. More than 98 percent of non-elderly, non-disabled NYCHA voucher tenants are single-parent households, and only a third of the parents work. The average time they spend in the program is over eight years, with more than a third of the recipients supported ten years or longer. The authority spends a staggering $700 million yearly in federal funds on the program and employs 740 people to administer it.

As large as NYCHA's Section 8 voucher population is, however, it represents little more than half of the city's total. New York's Department of Housing Preservation and Development administers an additional 25,000 Section 8s, chiefly in apartments that Gotham has helped renovate, at the expense of city taxpayers, whose hefty federal taxes already help support HUD. State government and the regional HUD office manage another 57,000 Section 8s in the city, in complexes such as East New York's Starrett City. In total, New York City, with 172,000 Section 8s of one kind or another, not only has more voucher tenants than any other city; it has more than any state, save California, with a population vastly greater than Gotham's.

The Section 8 universe is expanding all over the country, not just in New York. Since 1998, the overall federal budget for housing vouchers has rocketed 167 percent, from $6 billion to $16 billion. Section 8s consume 51 percent of the entire HUD budget, up from 36 percent five years ago, and the 2.1 million households now holding vouchers nationally far outnumber the 1.3 million households in public housing proper. In some cities—Chicago most notably—housing vouchers have actually replaced much of the public housing system, as housing authorities have "vouchered out" tenants and bulldozed notoriously blighted high-rise projects. . . .

Promoting Dependency

A major social benefit of a private rental market is its promotion of responsible behavior. Tenants must establish a good credit history, save money for their security deposits, come with good references from employers, pay the rent on time, maintain their apartments decently, and keep an eye on their children to avoid eviction. Part of the support for the Section 8 program has rested on the belief that it will have similarly beneficial effects, thanks to its market component. But the Section 8 vouchers in reality establish nothing like a true private rental market and so have none of those good effects. On the contrary: just like the old welfare system, housing vouchers promote dependency and subsidize irresponsibility.

To begin with, the route to a housing voucher in New York, perversely, begins in that great school of dependency, the homeless shelter.

NYCHA gives families in the shelters highest priority for receiving apartment vouchers, viewing them as the neediest of

Subsidizing Blight

Ed Rutkowski, who heads a community development corporation working to revitalize [a Baltimore, Maryland,] neighborhood, bluntly calls Section 8 "a catalyst in neighborhood deterioration and ghetto expansion." Every day, Rutkowski says, he finds himself fighting the program's unintended consequences: neglected properties, persistent crime and a continual influx of dysfunctional families, some of whom have never lived outside of public housing.

Section 8 is supposed to deconcentrate poverty, but in Rutkowski's view, it actually reconcentrates it—in struggling neighborhoods such as his.

Christopher Swope, Governing, *May 2002.*

the needy. As an equally perverse result, no matter how many vouchers NYCHA hands out to shelter families, the number of families entering the shelters continues to rise, rocketing to 9,200 in 2003, up from 5,192 three years earlier. A NYCHA official characterizes the process as "feeding the monster"—an increased supply of subsidized housing boosts demand and spurs thousands of New York families, almost all of them headed by single mothers, to flood the shelters so that they can move to the head of the line to get vouchers. In other words, increased subsidized housing creates more homelessness.

Housing advocates charge that the influx simply reveals the full extent of New York City's grave housing crisis. But it's important to be clear about the situation of most of New York's "homeless" families. Almost none had been sleeping on the streets or in the tunnels of Grand Central Terminal before showing up at one of the city's emergency intake units, claiming homelessness. One former high-ranking official at the Department of Homeless Services (DHS) observes that, in her six years at the agency, she knew "maybe three or four families who were sleeping at bus stations and that sort of thing."

A Slippery Definition

In fact, thanks in part to a court order that requires New York to provide permanent housing to any homeless person—the presumption that anyone declaring himself as such deserves the benefit of the doubt—"homeless" has become a slippery term in the city, its meaning based on the quality of a family's living arrangements rather than whether or not it has a roof over it. The DHS's Eligibility Investigation Unit will classify a household arriving at a shelter "homeless" simply because it finds their living arrangements "not appropriate," says DHS spokesman Jim Anderson. He explains: "That could involve the number of people and the number of rooms for sleeping, the sleeping arrangements—such as the age and gender and relationship of those sharing common sleeping rooms." Or, he adds, "it could involve fire safety or the possibility of domestic violence."

What this amounts to in practice, say those familiar with DHS procedures, is that the department frequently declares inappropriate a relatively commonplace situation in which a new teen mother, still living at home with her mother or grandmother until her baby's presence sparks a family fight, runs off to seek shelter as "homeless"—in order to get herself moved into a government-subsidized first home. It is common wisdom among NYCHA officials that many families moving from the shelter system into Section 8 apartments are headed by single mothers who are getting their own apartment for the first time, though there are no hard numbers to prove it. Nationally, HUD reports that more than 16,000 applicants under 21 receive housing vouchers every year.

The whole process—from shelter to Section 8 apartment—seems purposely designed to force into dependency those it claims to help. NYCHA, for example, runs semiweekly briefings for new voucher holders. Some of the young recipients show up with their mothers, who help them fill out the forms; the meetings remind one of a school orientation, except that here the "students" are being acculturated into dependency instead of getting ready to learn. There's no need for the parental help, as it turns out. Efficient NYCHA officials (and NYCHA is one of the most efficiently run housing authorities in the nation) are there to hold the voucher recipient's hand every step of the way: "Here's your voucher number"; "Meet your 'housing assistant'"; "These are the best days for appointments if you have problems with your landlord." . . .

Once a voucher holder is ensconced in a Section 8 apartment, the program then mires her even further in dependency, because all its incentives tell her not to improve her situation. Because Section 8 rent is pegged at 30 percent of income, any increase in a recipient's wages leads to a dishearteningly steep rent increase. If she gets a job that boosts her income from $10,000 to $15,000, her rent zooms from $250 to $375 a month. In effect, she's taxed as if she were well-off, at a marginal rate of 30 percent. (Conversely, Section 8 rents go down—potentially to next to nothing—if someone loses or quits a job or her welfare runs out.) Nor does getting married to a job holder necessarily make much economic sense. By pushing the household's income too high, it could cause her to lose the voucher benefit entirely.

Less-than-Model Tenants

Voucher recipients are drawn almost exclusively from the ranks of the city's most disorganized families and individuals, so it's hardly surprising that many do not conduct themselves as model tenants. "Section 8 tenants are much more difficult to deal with," says Mark Engel, president of Langsam Property Services Corporation, which rents out 1,700 Section 8 apartments in five- and six-story apartment buildings throughout the Bronx. "The families are fragmented. There are no husbands, and so there's not as much control over the children. So there are more damages—graffiti, breaking appliances, leaving garbage out in the hallways, breaking the entranceway door." Another Bronx landlord, who leases 700 apartments to Section 8 tenants, agrees. "A lot of those most eligible for the subsidy," he says, "are the least appreciative and the least sensitive to their obligations as tenants—either to owners or their neighbors." They can create truly bad environments. "I'm dealing right now with a tenant, a 29-year-old single mother with five kids and one on the way," he offers by way of example. "There's loud music, teenagers congregating in the hall. The apartment's in chaotic shape—hygiene bad, housekeeping a disaster."

Yet another Bronx property manager tells the story of a Section 8 tenant whose smoke detector went off, prompting her to knock it down with a broom, resulting in the apartment failing to pass NYCHA's annual inspection. Such carelessly inflicted damage is common: NYCHA reports that 18.5 percent of apartments inspected when a new voucher tenant moves in fail reinspection just one year later. Landlords are then obligated to make the repairs and bill the tenants. "Good luck getting them to pay," Engel says resignedly. And, he reports, almost a third of his voucher tenants neglect to chip in even their small share of the rent on time every month.

Faced with disruptive Section 8 neighbors—who sometimes include drug addicts or alcoholics from the city's homeless shelters—normal rent-paying tenants can become demoralized. "Too many people are negatively affected by some of the recipients," says a Section 8 landlord. "Tell me: where's the fairness to other tenants when they're forced to live with people who are not appropriately prepared for independent living?" NYCHA regularly receives letters from tenants complaining about voucher holders dealing drugs, causing excessive noise, or failing to supervise their children.

The misbehavior of many Section 8 tenants exposes the false assumption behind all subsidized housing: that providing the disorganized poor with low-cost but quality housing will uplift them. It's not the better environment that encourages someone to advance; it's the hard work and good life decisions that make for the better environment. For all the genial faith of Section 8's market-oriented creators, voucher tenants appear more likely to degrade their environment than their environment to uplift them.

> "It's more cost-efficient—and humane—to provide [the chronic homeless] a long-term residence up front and assign them visiting case workers."

Permanent Housing Will Reduce Chronic Homelessness

Christian Science Monitor

In the following viewpoint the editors of the Christian Science Monitor, *a national daily newspaper, claim that providing permanent housing is the best way to reduce chronic homelessness. The chronic homeless—the 10 percent of homeless Americans who spend years on the street—consume a majority of the resources spent on homelessness, the authors argue. Ferrying the chronic homeless through shelters, detox facilities, jails, and emergency rooms is expensive, the authors maintain. Providing the chronic homeless with housing and coordinated mental health and social services, they assert, is less costly and has proved successful.*

As you read, consider the following questions:

1. What did a Dayton, Ohio, study find when it moved a group of mentally ill homeless into an apartment building, according to the *Monitor*?
2. What have task forces to end chronic homelessness found, in the authors' view?
3. According to the authors, what are the two fastest-growing homeless groups?

From New York to San Francisco, the nation has arrived at a collective aha moment about how to reduce chronic homelessness. Instead of just trying to manage this entrenched problem, cities are aiming to end it, and they're making laudable headway.

People who may live for years on and off the street are not the largest part of the homeless population; they are only about 10 percent. But they are far more expensive and difficult for a city to deal with than other kinds of homeless. Often mentally ill or addicted to drugs or alcohol, the long-term homeless shuttle between the street, shelters, detox centers, jails, and emergency rooms.

A More Cost-Efficient Approach

What cities are discovering is that it's more cost-efficient—and humane—to provide these individuals a long-term residence up front and assign them visiting case workers, rather than allowing them to rack up hefty tabs as "frequent fliers" to city and private services.

Dayton, Ohio, for instance, has found that on the street, one group of mentally ill homeless individuals cost taxpayers $203 a day. But when they were moved into a 10-unit apartment building, with supportive health services, that cost dropped to $85 a day.

Dayton is part of a recent federal-led assault on chronic homelessness. It's spearheaded by the Interagency Council on

Helping the Chronically Homeless

Pouring billions of dollars into the homeless-shelter system does a lot for those who need time to relocate after they are forced to leave their homes. It also provides food to the hungry and a warm shelter in the winter. But this money fails to help the chronically homeless, the people who need shelter for more than the typical 90-day maximum stay at facilities, and who need help breaking their drinking habits.

Theresa Kennelly; University of Michigan Daily, *June 12, 2006.*

Homelessness, whose director, Philip Mangano, is taking a business-school approach to the problem. "Cost-benefit analysis is a friend to the homeless," he has said.

More than 200 cities and other jurisdictions have started 10-year plans, promoted by Mr. Mangano's council, to actually end chronic homelessness. They're getting community buy-in by including just about everyone on their task forces: businesses, foundations, religious groups, the media, and, of course, social services. They've had to identify the long-term homeless, then track them down one by one. They've found that a stable residence, individual attention, and a certain independence are helping people turn around their lives, with some finding jobs and contributing to rent.

Called "housing first," this approach differs from the more costly, managing-the-problem strategy of the mid-1980s. Then, cities built shelters tied to health services, with the hope that after the homeless stabilized, they would find long-term residences. But some spurned group shelters, or never stabilized.

Early returns show that the "housing first" approach to chronic homelessness is having an impact. In total, 30 of the 200-plus jurisdictions have reported homeless declines (some in chronic populations, others in their general homeless count). Since success breeds success, this should encourage cities to stick to their plans. It won't be easy to actually realize the savings because government agencies are loath to give up budget dollars—even ones they no longer need.

At the same time, these cities, as well as the federal government, should redouble efforts for the remaining 90 percent of the homeless. Two of the fastest growing homeless groups are the working poor and women with children (now, sadly, children make up a quarter of that vulnerable population).

Finally, the nation is making progress on homelessness. But it must become a 100-percent effort.

> *"It is in everyone's best interests to avoid passing a law that seeks to end homelessness among one population by worsening homelessness among another."*

Programs That Focus on Chronic Homelessness Will Hurt Homeless Families

Gloria M. Guard

Funding programs that focus on ending chronic homelessness threaten programs that help the fastest-growing homeless population—families—argues Gloria M. Guard in the following viewpoint. Homelessness has a devastating impact on children who, due to developmental delays and personal trauma, are at risk of becoming homeless as adults, she maintains. Homeless families need job and life skills training programs that funding the more visible chronic homeless will erode, she claims. Guard is president of the People's Emergency Center, a homeless family service provider in Philadelphia, Pennsylvania.

As you read, consider the following questions:

1. According to Guard, how did Congress single out homeless families in 1987?

Gloria M. Guard, "Written Statement of Gloria M. Guard, Submitted to the Subcommittee on Housing and Transportation of the Senate Committee on Banking, Housing, and Urban Affairs, Hearing on S. 1801, the Community Partnership to End Homelessness Act," March 30, 2006. Reproduced by permission.

2. How are the chronic homeless defined, in the author's opinion?

3. In Guard's view, what has two decades of on-the-ground experience shown about family homelessness?

A ction without due caution can be a recipe for disaster. And [homeless family service providers in Philadelphia] believe that [the Community Partnership to End Homelessness Act, a reauthorization of the McKinney-Vento Homeless Assistance Act] in its current form would be potentially catastrophic to the nation's homeless families and children. Congress has long regarded homeless families to be an especially vulnerable segment of the nation's homeless population and, as such, singled them out as requiring special attention when McKinney-Vento was enacted into law in 1987. Congress clearly recognized the unique and compelling needs of homeless families and children, and for obvious good reason. It is impossible to ignore the devastating impact that long-term and short-term homelessness have on young children. Two decades ago McKinney-Vento rightly placed a "special emphasis" on assisting "families with children" by mandating that not less than one quarter of funds be "allocated to projects designed primarily to serve homeless families with children."

Reducing Assistance for Homeless Families

And yet, nearly 20 years later, with evidence showing that families are the fastest-growing subset of the homeless population in the United States, with evidence mounting that many homeless children become tomorrow's homeless adults, we are being asked to consider a Congressional reauthorization that *consistently reduces assistance for homeless families.* This proposed bill contains key funding mandates, bonuses and legislative language that would severely erode funding for the homeless families who come to us daily seeking help. . . . When components of this bill are taken as a whole the legislation would have the *net effect of terminating funding for well-*

A Need to Expand Eligibility

The Samaritan Initiative [Act of 2004, which as of November 2006 remained in committee] relies on a definition of "chronically homeless person" that categorically excludes families with children, even families with disabled members who have suffered from repeated or extended periods of homelessness. This artificial exclusion, combined with the policy changes being advanced by HUD, will hinder the efforts of homeless service providers to assist many homeless families with children in their struggle to achieve stability. We therefore propose that eligibility be expanded to include families with a disabled adult or child.

James Mauck, congressional testimony, July 13, 2004.

established services that have long helped homeless families achieve self-sufficiency. This bill would preclude its core goal of prevention. If we are serious about "ending homelessness," surely we must consider today's homeless children and intervene now before they become tomorrow's homeless adults.

Senator [Jack] Reed's proposed bill has many strengths, including a heavy emphasis on outcomes and quality control, a streamlined funding application process, and an acknowledgment of a role for transitional housing which we wholeheartedly support. It also has some promising provisions that we would support *if strengthened*, such as the provision allowing program funds to be used for permanent housing for families where no member has a disability. It also is informed by a promising theoretical framework. But experience already has shown that this laudable theory does not play out in practice as it is intended to.

The proposed legislation would require localities to spend a large percentage of money they receive from the U.S. Department of Housing and Urban Development [HUD] on a very small but needy population—the so-called "chronic homeless." By definition, members of this group are disabled, have extreme drug/alcohol addictions and/or suffer from severe mental illnesses. Generally speaking, these are the people we see on the streets and in the subways of our largest cities. Key elements of the bill have already been implemented by HUD and so far we have seen that this "chronic homeless initiative" can be financed only by taking money away from other homeless populations—namely, families, who have the political disadvantage of being a much less visible but no less needy group.

Collateral Damage

Supporters of the bill offer no effective remedy for this inherent flaw in the policy, even though the very real ramifications have begun to show in cities such as Philadelphia, where incremental HUD policy shifts have been underway for several years now without Congressional mandate. Collateral damage reportedly is playing out as far away as Colorado, Illinois and Rhode Island as well. In [2005], providers such as my own agency, People's Emergency Center, have lost millions of HUD dollars collectively for programs that largely assist homeless families—job-training, life skills, parent education and counseling programs that many homeless parents and children need.

It is intellectually and empirically dishonest to declare that such supportive services and transitional housing support are unnecessary for many families. That wrongly assumes that the majority of homeless families in our country need only "plain vanilla affordable housing"—an extraordinary statement made to this same panel during a hearing four years ago. Although the idea of "vanilla affordable housing" may be tempting to swallow, the reality of two decades of on-the-ground experience has shown that family homelessness is not a one-dimensional problem of housing affordability. Prevention for this group often requires more than simply a rental subsidy, a security deposit or an affordable housing unit. Prevention requires the services needed to transition to self-sufficiency and housing stability. Prevention requires that homeless children receive the educational and emotional supports needed to prevent lifelong developmental delays and traumas that put them at risk of becoming homeless adults.

We realize that it has been challenging for architects of this bill to effectively engage the hundreds if not thousands of homeless family assistance agencies nationwide in weighing provisions that would strike the right balance to ending homelessness. We commend Senator Reed's office for toiling so long on this important bill and we are eager to be a part of the continuing dialogue about how it should look. Surely, it is in everyone's best interests to *avoid* passing a law that seeks to end homelessness among one population by worsening homelessness among another. Balance is essential to any comprehensive policy to end homelessness. As family specialists, we cannot understate the negative impact the Community Partnership to End Homelessness Act would have on communities small and large if not substantially altered before becoming law.[1]

1. As of November 2006, this bill remains in committee.

Periodical Bibliography

The following articles have been selected to supplement the diverse views presented in this chapter.

America	"More Homeless, Less Housing," February 28, 2005.
Boston Globe	"The Shelter Threshold," April 4, 2006.
David Cho	"For More Suburban Families, Affordable Housing Elusive," *Washington Post*, April 15, 2003.
Kevin Fagan	"A Way Out," *San Francisco Chronicle*, December 2, 2003.
Jeffrey M. Jones	"Homeless No More?" *Weekly Standard*, June 20, 2005.
Theresa Kennelly	"Chronically Homeless," *University of Michigan Daily*, June 12, 2006.
Los Angeles Times	"A Place to Call Their Own," May 4, 2006.
Los Angeles Times	"Not in Their Backyard," May 4, 2006.
Jeffrey G. MacDonald	"Homelessness Should Be Treated as a Human Rights Violation, Argue Housing Advocates," *Christian Science Monitor*, February 4, 2004.
Terry Philpot	"From Hotel to Home: New York's Non-Profit Housing and Community Developments Have Been a Great Success," *Nursing Standard*, August 31, 2005.
Marianna Riley	"Solution, Not Shelters," *St. Louis Post-Dispatch*, March 9, 2004.
Seattle Post-Intelligencer	"Homelessness: Housing for All," August 28, 2005.
William Tucker	"Give 'Em Shelter; Good News for the Homeless," *Weekly Standard*, July 3, 2006.

OPPOSING
VIEWPOINTS®
SERIES

CHAPTER 4

What Policies Will Best Reduce Homelessness?

Chapter Preface

Cities across the United States have enacted local ordinances to regulate activities that affect the homeless. A Dallas, Texas, law makes it a crime to "sleep or doze in a street, alley, park, or other public place." Some cities conduct sweeps in which the police selectively enforce loitering or open-container laws in areas where homeless people gather, particularly in anticipation of public events. Atlanta, Georgia, for example, selectively enforced criminal trespass and panhandling laws in preparation for the Olympic Games. Other communities enact laws that punish people for begging or panhandling. Cleveland, Ohio, for example, passed a law that prohibits panhandling within twenty feet of an ATM, bus stop, or sidewalk café. A few cities penalize those offering outdoor feedings for homeless individuals. A Dallas ordinance penalizes charities, churches, and other organizations that serve food to the needy outside of particularly designated areas, and those who violate this ordinance can be fined up to $2000. One of many controversies in the homelessness debate is whether these ordinances criminalize homelessness or instead are necessary to protect public health and safety.

City officials who support these ordinances claim that these laws are necessary to protect the health and safety of those who live, work, and visit the community. In addition, officials argue, these laws reduce the negative economic impact of panhandlers and those sleeping on the streets. For example, the stated purpose of a Seattle, Washington, statute that prohibits sitting or lying on a public sidewalk is "to facilitate the safe and efficient movement of pedestrians and goods . . . to eliminate public safety hazard[s], and to protect the economic health and productivity of commercial areas." Some officials stress that these measures should be combined with efforts to help the homeless. In early 2006, for example, San

Francisco, California, threatened with arrest the homeless camping in Golden Gate Park in violation of a local ordinance. The order gave the homeless time to remove their belongings and paired them with social workers who advised them on how to find housing. "If [public sleeping] is negatively impacting a neighborhood, we are going to deal with it," said Trent Rhorer, the city's head of human services, "but deal with it sensitively and responsibly in a way that gets people in real services instead of simply fining them, citing them and putting them in jail."

Critics claim that these laws criminalize homelessness and violate constitutional rights. Antipanhandling ordinances, these analysts argue, infringe on the right to free speech under the First Amendment. In *Loper v. New York City Police Dept.*, for example, the court ruled that begging is protected speech because it usually involves the communication of a "social or political message." The message in *Loper*, the court ruled, is "the need for food, shelter, transportation or medical care." Some courts have found that arresting the homeless for sleeping outside when no shelter is available violates their Eighth Amendment right to be free from cruel and unusual punishment. In *Porringer*, sleeping outside, the activity for which the plaintiffs were arrested, was "inseparable from their involuntary condition of being homeless." Thus, the court reasons, "as long as the homeless plaintiffs do not have a single place where they can lawfully be, the challenged ordinances, as applied to them, effectively punish them for something for which they may not be convicted under the Eighth Amendment—sleeping, eating, and other innocent conduct."

Whether laws that target the homeless protect public safety or criminalize the homeless remains controversial. The authors of the viewpoints in the following chapter debate other issues to answer the question, What policies will best reduce homelessness?

> *"New [federal] initiatives will result in visible, measurable, and quantifiable change in our communities, on our streets, and in the lives of homeless people."*

Government Initiatives Can Reduce Homelessness

Philip F. Mangano

Government homelessness initiatives will visibly and measurably reduce homelessness, claims Philip F. Mangano in the following viewpoint. Since 1987, he asserts, the government has spent valuable resources managing homelessness. This approach, he argues, has failed to help the chronic homeless—the 10 percent of the homeless population who consume 50 percent of the resources. Instead, he maintains, the government should spend its resources getting these people off the street. Mangano is executive director of the United States Interagency Council on Homelessness (ICH).

As you read, consider the following questions:

1. In Mangano's opinion, what supportive housing strategies sustain tenancies?

Philip F. Mangano, "Testimony before the House VA/HUD/Independent Agencies Appropriations Subcommittee," March 17, 2004.

2. According to the author, what is the price of waiting for at-risk populations to become homeless?

3. How does Mangano explain his assertion that homelessness is a national problem with local solutions?

The [United States Interagency] Council [on Homelessness] is establishing a new standard of expectation for the investment of federal homeless resources. That expectation is that our new initiatives will result in visible, measurable, and quantifiable change in our communities, on our streets, and in the lives of homeless people. Billions of dollars have been spent on homeless programs since the enactment of the McKinney Act in 1987. Research tells us that there are now more than 40,000 homeless programs around the country. Yet despite all this investment of resources over the last twenty years, there have been and continue to be thousands of people experiencing chronic homelessness living on the streets and in encampments in our communities and long term in our shelters. To get a different result, our investments must be guided by a management agenda that prioritizes results.

The "verb" of homelessness needs to be changed. For 20 years, we have been "managing" the problem; now [the George W. Bush] Administration is working to end the disgrace of chronic homelessness. To achieve different results, the Council staff and its member agencies are implementing the President's Management Agenda, which calls for investments and policies to be research and data driven and performance-based.

Understanding Chronic Homelessness

The President's FY [fiscal year] 2005 proposed Samaritan Initiative is part of the Administration's larger effort to end chronic homelessness—a goal that is directly driven by research that shows this is a problem the can be solved. Chronic homelessness is the most visible form of homelessness in our country, and is most often a result of disabilities. This form of homelessness, often finding its expression on the streets of our communities, is cited by the public, the media, community leaders, neighborhood groups, Chambers of Commerce, downtown business districts, and others as demanding a response. Seemingly intractable, chronic homelessness has been addressed by communities across the nation that have attempted ad hoc responses with little evidence of long-term success.

Over the last few years a body of research has been developed that tells us that those experiencing chronic homelessness are a finite group representing only 10% of the homeless population. They, however, consume over 50% of all emergency homeless services and ricochet around the acute side of very expensive health care systems. As a result, they are some of the most expensive people in social service systems.

Cost-Effective Housing Strategies

Most importantly, the research tells us that there are interventions that are not only effective in ending the homelessness of individuals who have been living long term on the streets and in shelters but which can be cost effective. Research shows that supportive housing strategies, such as multidisciplinary, clinically-based engagement with housing and appropriate supportive services, help to sustain tenancies. These models of housing, along with other models, can be effective in moving chronically homeless persons off the streets and out of shelters into sustainable tenancies and toward recovery and self-sufficiency. Outcomes of different models of supportive housing efforts in New York City, Columbus, Ohio and San Francisco, demonstrate a strong success rate of housing stability and retention for those most vulnerable and long-term shelter and street inhabitants.

The research shows chronically homeless persons not only spend significant periods of time living on the streets and in other public spaces, they also cycle repeatedly through a variety of expensive community care systems, including shelters and correctional and emergency health-care facilities. One study of nearly 5,000 homeless persons with severe mental disorders in New York City found that they had used an average of over $34,000 a year in publicly funded hospitalization and correctional services.

A New Direction

Learning from—and acting on—what the research shows has given us a policy direction. That policy direction is embodied in the Samaritan Initiative, which would provide authority for the Departments of Housing and Urban Development [HUD], Health and Human Services [HHS], and Veterans Affairs [VA] to jointly fund community-based efforts to coordinate the provision of housing with supportive services, including health care, mental health, and substance abuse treatment services to move chronically homeless persons from the streets and out of shelters into permanent housing with the supportive services available to sustain those tenancies. The President's budget requests $70 million in new resources for this competitive grants initiative—$50 million from HUD, $10 million from HHS, and $10 million through the VA Medical Care account. VA involvement ensures that chronically homeless veterans can be identified, engaged, and referred to the appropriate VA services.

The Samaritan Initiative is a performance-based program intended to result in a visible and quantifiable reduction in the number of chronically homeless persons living on the streets and long term in shelters. Grantees would be expected to quantify the reduction in the number of chronically homeless persons.

Preventing Homelessness

In addition to the Samaritan Initiative, which is an intervention strategy in the lives of those who are experiencing chronic homelessness that works to end homelessness through innova-

A Worthy Goal

Clearly, the challenge of ending homelessness is a formidable one. But cities and states around the country have taken up the challenge to develop and implement plans to end homelessness. . . . Even the federal government has gotten on board. . . . The [George W.] Bush administration proposed ending chronic homelessness in ten years.

Ending homelessness won't solve the housing crisis. It won't end poverty. What it can do is ensure that everyone in our nation has a roof over their heads so that they can move on to the other business at hand. Isn't that a worthy goal of the best-housed nation in the world?

Nan Roman,
Housing Facts & Findings (Fannie Mae Foundation), 2002.

tive engagement and housing strategies, the Council has also focused on prevention of homelessness. To accomplish the Administration's objective to end chronic homelessness in the next decade, the Council has reprioritized prevention in the national strategy. Waiting for at-risk populations to fall into homelessness only creates more homeless specific programs, increases costs, and deepens the human tragedy.

The Council seeks to coordinate a more comprehensive strategy that includes intervention and prevention. To that end, the Administration continues its investment in mainstream prevention resources in the FY 05 budget including resources targeted to emerging populations that could fall into homelessness, including funding targeted to prevention and better outcomes for ex-prisoners, and young adults aging out of foster care. Deeper investments in mental health services and substance abuse treatment capacity will also have a preventative impact.

The Council has also worked to ensure that prevention is made tangible through improved discharge planning strategies and protocols at the federal, state and local levels. These strategies are evident in the state interagency councils and community 10-Year Plans fostered by the Council.

In fashioning a national response to preventing and ending chronic homelessness, the Council is establishing partnerships between federal agencies, state houses, city halls and county executive offices, downtown associations, Chambers of Commerce, faith-based and community organizations, the United Way, providers and advocates, and homeless people themselves. The Council recognizes that homelessness is a national problem with local solutions. No one federal agency, no one level of government and no one sector of the community can reach the goal alone. Federal agency collaborations and partnerships with state and local governments and the private and faith-based and community sectors are key to achieving the objectives of preventing and ending chronic homelessness. . . .

Identifying Innovative Initiatives

The Council has held a number of national focus groups to inform our policy deliberations and identify best practices and innovative programs that are achieving the desired outcomes of preventing and ending homelessness and that can be replicated in other communities. Prior focus groups have focused on rural homelessness, family homelessness, innovative housing solutions, and faith-based initiatives. Future focus groups are planned on youth homelessness, research, state interagency council development and implementation, implementation of community 10-Year Plans to end chronic homelessness, and technical assistance.

In conjunction with the Council's work with communities in the development of 10-Year Plans, the Council has held regional focus groups bringing together city and county administrators from 180 communities. Innovative practitioners from around the country and city officials from communities whose plans are already underway served as faculty. The impact of these focus groups was to encourage many communities to engage in 10-year planning processes and to disseminate information on results-oriented, evidence-based practices across the country. . . .

The Continuing Work of the Council

The Council intends to continue its statutory activities of: 1) federal homeless program coordination, 2) governmental and private programs evaluation, 3) information distribution, and 4) provision of technical assistance. Additionally, the Council will continue to foster new collaborative prevention and intervention opportunities among federal agencies as well as monitor those initiatives already underway to document outcomes and identify best practices.

The Council will continue to work with federal, state and local agencies to strengthen partnerships. Our goal . . . is that every state and territory will develop a state interagency council on homelessness, and that more than 100 cities and counties will create and implement 10-Year Plans to end chronic homelessness.

The Council will continue to develop the ICH website as the central federal website on homelessness and will work with member agencies to improve navigation to homelessness information on their sites.

Since its revitalization in March 2002, the 20 member agencies that comprise the Council and the Council staff have taken an approach to homelessness that is based on accountability, collaboration and results. We believe that our approach to strengthen prevention programs and to fund performance-based, results-oriented interventions will produce a visible reduction in homelessness in this country.

*"We spend more and more on the home-
less, and still their numbers increase."*

Government Initiatives Will Not Reduce Homelessness

John Derbyshire

*In the following viewpoint John Derbyshire argues that the fed-
eral government should not be in the business of helping the
homeless. In fact, he reasons, giving government handouts to the
homeless only increases homelessness. Indeed, Derbyshire asserts,
homeless numbers continue to grow despite government spending. The problem of homelessness should be left to private charity, he claims, except, of course, for those who require special services, such as the mentally ill. Derbyshire, a British-born author,
is a columnist for the conservative magazine* National Review.

As you read, consider the following questions:

1. What experience precipitated Derbyshire's observations
   about the problem of homelessness?
2. How did neighboring towns and counties respond to the
   author's editorial decrying the money San Francisco
   gave its vagrants?

John Derbyshire, "Throw the Bums Out: But Do So with Compassion—Coolidge Style
Compassion," *National Review*, vol. 55, issue 12, June 30, 2003. Copyright © 2003 by
National Review, Inc., 215 Lexington Avenue, New York, NY 10016. Reproduced by
permission.

3. What was expected of recipients of private charity before the present, humanitarian age, in Derbyshire's view?

On a recent business trip to San Francisco I decided to take a look at the new Asian Art Museum, which is in the old municipal library building, on one side of the downtown Civic Center Plaza. The museum is very impressive; but in making my way to it on foot across the downtown area, I acquired impressions of a different kind, which affected other senses beside the visual. I encountered San Francisco's appalling vagrancy problem.

It is in the downtown area that the problem is most obvious. I have never seen so many street people in one place. Crossing the plaza to the museum I found myself weaving my way through platoons, companies, battalions of them. Here a ragged, emaciated woman mumbling to herself and making complicated hand gestures like a Buddhist priest; there a huge black-bearded Rasputin of a man in a floor-length heavy overcoat, pushing a shopping cart piled high with filthy bundles; across the way a little knot of florid winos arguing loudly and ferociously about something; sitting on the sidewalk where I passed, a youngish black woman, gaunt and nearly bald, with some sort of horrid skin disease all over her face and scalp, croaking something at me I couldn't understand.

Colonizing Public Spaces

As I said, the Asian Art Museum is housed in the old municipal library. There is a $10 door fee, so the vagrants do not enter. On the other side of the plaza, however, is a spiffy new library, built at a cost of $137 million. It has practically been colonized by the street people. Defying the best efforts of a state-of-the-art air-conditioning system, the tang of unwashed bodies pervades the place. One row of computers (like all modern libraries, the new San Francisco municipal is long on computers and short on books . . .) is occupied entirely by vagrants watching DVD movies. One of them has his feet, clad in filthy sneakers, up on the desk. I got chatting with a security guard, a fellow in the last weary stages of cynicism.

He took me to the security office and showed me their "gallery"—an entire wall covered with polaroid snapshots of library patrons apprehended for various offenses. The snapshots were arranged by offense category, each category tagged with a three-digit police code. The guard interpreted the codes for me. "These are the assaults . . . here you have the substance abusers . . . these here were defacing the books . . ." I pointed to a block of 40 or 50 photographs he'd missed. What had their offense been? "Oh, those are the masturbators."

A block east of the museum is U.N. Plaza, boasting a modern-style fountain—a sprawling arrangement of granite slabs and water jets, designed by a world-famous architect. This has naturally proved irresistible to the armies of vagrants. For years they urinated, defecated, and discarded drug paraphernalia there—the last to such a degree that the water was dangerous with chemical contaminants, even if you could bring yourself to ignore the waste products. The city's Department of Public Works used to conduct a daily clean-up. Early [in 2003], though, they decided that the cost was more than could be justified. In March [2003], a chain-link fence was erected around the whole thing, in the teeth of, it goes without saying, vehement protests from "advocates for the homeless." (The word "homeless" is the current euphemism for vagrants, publicized by activist New York attorney Robert Hayes in the early 1980s.)

Funding the Homeless

It is not too hard to figure out why San Francisco has so many vagrants. Indigent adults receive cash payments of $320 to $395 a month, with only a nominal work requirement for the able-bodied. Supplemented by a little panhandling, this is a tidy sum in the agreeable Northern California climate. When I wrote about the situation on [the *National Review*] website,

The Problem with One-Sided Giving

Politicians agree that this one-sided giving is unhealthy. In their rhetoric, they condemn policies of "handout," and extol the virtues of the "helping hand." Yet in practice, program after program turns into another dependency-causing subsidy.

Nowhere is this pattern more dramatically illustrated than in programs to provide shelter for the unhoused. Governments keep increasing their efforts, only to reap ever-growing numbers of homeless.

James L. Payne, Freeman, August 1992.

I got e-mails from people in neighboring towns and counties saying: "Please don't write about this. We're happy with things just as they are. San Francisco takes in all our homeless people, so we're spared the problem. . . ."

Naturally this logic is lost on the city's irredeemably liberal Board of Supervisors and their soulmates in the local press. One of the latter, Ilene Leichuk of the *San Francisco Chronicle*, recently began a sentence thus: "With San Francisco's homeless population growing despite the millions of dollars the city spends annually to help its most desperate residents . . ." Note that word "despite." We spend more and more on the homeless, and still their numbers increase. How can this be? What a strange and wonderful thing is the liberal mind! (Recall the similarly clueless *New York Times* headline: "Crime Keeps on Falling, but Prisons Keep on Filling.")

By [2002] the situation had already got so bad that city voters were presented with a November ballot initiative, Proposition N, under whose terms that $395 monthly cash handout would be reduced to $59, the balance being replaced by city-provided food and shelter. This "Care not Cash" initiative was

passed, with 60 percent of voters in favor. That of course out-
raged the city's left-wing activists, who immediately challenged the vote in court. On May 8 Superior Court judge
Ronald Quidachay ruled that only the Board of Supervisors
can set city welfare policy, and that the ballot initiative was
therefore invalid. The hundred-dollar-a-week handouts to
anyone who shows up will continue—in a city that is looking
at a $350 million deficit [in 2003].

Compassion, Not Handouts

The United States of America was founded on the notion of
self-support, of people taking care of their families, joining
with neighbors to solve common problems in a humane and
sensible way. Those common problems would include the occasional citizen, like Huckleberry Finn's pap, who could not,
or stubbornly would not, look after himself, and for whom
some public provision should be made. When a person "came
upon the town," the town would give him some minimal aid,
while of course private citizens, if they felt inclined, could exercise the virtue of private charity to any degree they wished.
The recipient was, however, expected to defer to community
standards. If he persistently committed gross violations of
those standards—relieving himself in the town fountain would
certainly have counted—he was locked up or institutionalized.

This was a sound system, widely admired outside our borders. Listen to the most American of American presidents,
Calvin Coolidge: "The principle of service is not to be con-
fused with a weak and impractical sentimentalism." "Self-
government means self-support." "The normal must care for
themselves."

There was nothing callous about this attitude. Everyone
understood that the feeble-minded and insane needed special
care in state institutions. (The famously parsimonious
Coolidge made a speech in 1916, when he was lieutenant gov-
ernor of Massachusetts, defending the robust state funding of

insane asylums.) Our present age, for all its humanitarian cant, is much crueler. Nationwide, 39 percent of vagrants have some diagnosable mental-health problem—victims, for the most part, of the deinstitutionalization that began after the 1963 Community Mental Health Centers Act. Crueler, and also more careless of the dignity and independence of the individual. That applies not only to the individual vagrant, but to the self-supporting citizen, too. As you cross Civic Center Plaza they leer at you, yell at you, sometimes harass you. If you are a woman, they make lewd remarks at you. All this we are supposed to put up with in the name of "compassion" and "rights." And put up with it we do! Why?

> *"HUD should be funded to distribute 100,000 or more one- or two-year housing vouchers to the neediest of Katrina's homeless victims."*

Housing Vouchers Will Help Homeless Hurricane Katrina Victims

Bruce Katz and Mark Muro

According to Bruce Katz and Mark Muro in the following viewpoint, policy makers should fund a housing voucher program for victims of Hurricane Katrina. Like the program that successfully helped victims of the Northridge, California, earthquake in 1994, housing vouchers, a program that subsidizes rent payments, would allow hurricane victims to immediately begin rebuilding their lives. By providing hurricane victims with economic mobility, housing vouchers would also reduce the concentration of poverty that has plagued New Orleans. Katz is vice president and Muro policy director of the Brookings Institution's Metropolitan Policy Program.

Bruce Katz and Mark Muro, "To Shelter Katrina's Victims, Learn from the Northridge Quake Zone," *The Brookings Institution*, September 12, 2005. www.brookings.edu. Copyright 2005 Brookings Institution. Reproduced by permission.

As you read, consider the following questions:

1. According to Katz and Muro, how quickly did displaced Northridge earthquake victims begin to move into stable apartments?
2. In the authors' opinion, how many people in New Orleans lived in neighborhoods of extreme poverty?
3. What was the impact of New Orleans' concentration of poverty, in the author's view?

As the Gulf Coast struggles to respond to the magnitude of Hurricane Katrina's wrath—with some 700,000 Americans displaced and hundreds of thousands of homes devastated—the search is on for an aggressive, innovative, and rapid response to a housing catastrophe.

The good news is, one already exists.

A Proven Strategy

After the 1994 earthquake near Los Angeles, the federal Department of Housing and Urban Development [HUD] mounted an effort that was both successful and replicable. While the scale was smaller—20,000 Angelenos homeless, and over 55,000 residential structures damaged—a consensus approach emerged that brought the federal government, the state, landlords, and the region's leaders together to solve a massive problem.

The day after the quake, HUD was in L.A. with a plan that put the poorest victims on a path to recovery quickly and humanely. What happened next was unprecedented. Within days, Congress appropriated $200 milion to support a HUD plan to provide special Section 8 housing vouchers good for use anywhere in California.

Within a week, the first of 22,000 of the lowest-income displaced families were moving not into trailers and convention centers, but into stable apartments in safer and better neighborhoods than they had left.

Bridging the Gap

Tax credits are usually insufficient by themselves to reduce rents to the point where poor households can afford them. An additional subsidy normally is required to bridge that gap, and Section 8 housing vouchers are well suited to this purpose. Accordingly, Congress should provide housing authorities on the Gulf Coast with at least 13,500 additional "project-based" housing vouchers to be assigned to housing units financed with the new tax credits or to supportive housing units for people with disabilities financed with other capital funds. These 13,500 vouchers would enable 25 percent of the 54,000 rental units that can be constructed with the tax credits to be made available to poor families.

Will Fischer and Barbara Said,
Center on Budget and Policy Priorities, February 27, 2006.

And within a month, HUD had conducted a major landlord-recruitment forum to encourage landlords to take in quake victims.

In short, government intervened boldly and effectively in a shattered housing market to help the unhoused rebuild their lives through their own choices.

Compelling Gains

And now it should do so again. With more than half a million people homeless in the Gulf region, HUD should be funded to distribute 100,000 or more one- or two-year housing vouchers to the neediest of Katrina's homeless victims, just as it did . . . in Los Angeles.

The gains would be compelling. As much as the Federal Emergency Management Administration's cash assistance, vouchers would help hundreds of thousands of people quickly. Meanwhile, renewable certificates of one or two years' duration would buy families real stability for periods long enough to allow them to begin re-building their lives.

Nor do we have to create a new program to achieve these gains. One already exists. Currently HUD's Section 8 Housing Choice Voucher Program serves two million American families throughout the country and taps into a broad, capable, and preexisting network of housing agencies and private sector landlords—many located in areas now receiving families evacuated from the flood. With appropriate waivers to shorten administrative procedures and encourage landlords to take in voucher bearers, HUD could again turn its standard program into a powerful, rapid-response variant for use right now along the Gulf Coast.

Promoting Economic Mobility

Yet there is another advantage of such an approach. Employing housing vouchers on a massive scale responds to the crying need to promote residential and economic mobility and end the unacceptably sharp concentration of poverty that has for decades hobbled New Orleans' long-term prospects.

As the entire world now knows, New Orleans is one of the poorest cities in the United States. But it's the concentration of poverty—the bunching together of poor families in spatially isolated neighborhoods—that has the most pernicious impact on residents and the city.

Before the hurricane, about one in five poor people in New Orleans, and one in three poor blacks, lived in neighborhoods of extreme poverty with rates over 40 percent—the fifth-highest rate of concentrated poverty in the country. Dozens of census blocks had even higher concentrations.

While many of these families were the working poor—minimum wage workers employed by hotels and restaurants—many more were unemployed. Their neighborhoods—catch basins of poverty that were some of the first inundated in the rising flood waters—had always made it harder for residents to find jobs, because jobs tended to be elsewhere. And they made it difficult to educate their children, since schools and teachers were overwhelmed by the concentration of poor kids in the classroom.

More broadly, this concentration of poverty also crippled the ability of New Orleans to reach its true economic potential, because it stifled market investment, driving away the middle class and draining tax resources.

An infusion of housing vouchers, however, would give displaced residents from the city an opportunity they've never really had: to move to places—either near New Orleans or far away—that have plentiful jobs, good schools, and safe streets.

And that may prove critical to New Orleans' future as well. Supporting households in their quest for better neighborhoods, better jobs, and better schools would aid and abet the reinvention of New Orleans as a place of econonomically integrated communities with a healthier mix of quality housing, small businesses, and families located there by choice with a wider range of incomes.

In sum, Congress and the [George W.] Bush Administration have in their belt a housing tool—and tested in the Los Angeles earthquake—for remaking the social landscape of New Orleans and improving the lives of tens of thousands of the most destitute Americans across the Gulf Coast.

Will they use it?

> *"Over the long-term, [the voucher] approach seems likely to leave those families [displaced by Katrina] in just another place with high levels of poverty."*

Vouchers Are Inadequate to Help Many Homeless Hurricane Katrina Victims

Greg Anrig Jr.

Expanding the housing voucher program will not help Hurricane Katrina victims, maintains Greg Anrig Jr. in the following viewpoint. Housing vouchers subsidize the rent of low-income families, increasing economic mobility and reducing the concentration of poverty. However, Anrig argues, the subsidy will likely be modest and therefore keep victims concentrated in high-poverty neighborhoods, defeating the vouchers' purpose. Moreover, Anrig asserts, the time spent identifying those who are truly eligible will defeat the goal of getting victims into housing quickly. Anrig is vice president for programs at The Century Foundation, a center-left think tank.

As you read, consider the following questions:

1. According to Anrig, how do the numbers of Katrina victims differ from those in antipoverty efforts?

Greg Anrig Jr., "David Brooks Is Right, But . . . ," *The Century Foundation News & Commentary*, September 9, 2005. Reproduced by permission.

2. How were the awards to the survivors of 9/11 determined, according to the author?

3. In the author's view, what is the main reason why anti-poverty programs have not been emulated more widely?

David Brooks' [September 8, 2005, *New York Times*] column . . . uncharacteristically put forward a great idea. He argues that [Hurricane] Katrina creates a chance for the New Orleans residents who were trapped in high-poverty neighborhoods to resettle in mixed-income locations (including an intelligently rebuilt New Orleans)—where they and their children ultimately would have a much better chance of living a decent life. But what Brooks doesn't say is that making that "silver lining" a reality will require focused leadership from the president on down to state and local governments and private institutions, an enormous commitment of resources and effort, massive coordination, and political courage. So don't hold your breath.

Contrasting Circumstances

As Brooks mentions, studies of the Gautreaux and Moving to Opportunity programs[1], which provided housing vouchers to enable people to move from impoverished to middle-income neighborhoods, show much more positive outcomes than other anti-poverty efforts have produced (except the earned-income tax credit). The scale and nature of today's crisis is far different from the circumstances under which those programs were implemented, however. In both those cases, the participants all volunteered to move. In contrast to the hundreds of thousands suddenly displaced by Katrina the Gautreaux program affected 25,000 families over a long time span from 1976

1. The Gautreaux demonstration provided special-purpose vouchers and counseling to African American families who moved from poor, predominantly black neighborhoods in Chicago to racially integrated communities in the city and its suburbs. The Moving to Opportunity demonstration is a carefully controlled experiment to test the impacts of helping families move from high-poverty assisted housing projects to low-poverty neighborhoods.

to 1998 while about 4,200 families from five cities participated in Moving to Opportunity from 1994 to 1999. And both those programs were carefully designed with ample lead time.

So what would it take to make those two successful models work on a vastly larger scale in a time of crisis? The biggest challenge would be to provide housing vouchers to those displaced that would be sizeable enough to enable them to afford rent in middle-class neighborhoods, and to get landlords dispersed throughout such communities to accept them for an indefinite period. By way of [*Washington Monthly* journalist] Kevin Drum, the University of Virginia's Ed Olsen [an economist] recommends expanding HUD's Section 8 Housing Choice Voucher Program to enable those who have been displaced to move to locations in the south central U.S. with high rental vacancy rates. As a stopgap measure, that may be the best available alternative. But over the long-term, that approach seems likely to leave those families in just another place with high levels of poverty because the program's subsidies are so modest and so many new people would have to be absorbed in relatively concentrated locations. To do what Brooks is talking about would require a large premium above Section 8's subsidy level, along with all kinds of assistance to help people find space and be successfully integrated into middle-class communities.

A Larger Number of Victims

In thinking about how to fairly compensate those who have been displaced, a few numbers to keep in mind by way of perspective: according to a RAND study, awards from the September 11th Victims Compensation Fund created by Congress for the heirs of civilians killed (or those seriously injured) in the attacks that day ranged from $250,000 to $7.1 million and averaged $2.08 million. Adding in insurance benefits and charity, the average was $3.1 million per victim. (Of the total compensation, about 69 percent came from the Victim's Compen-

sation Fund, 23 percent from insurance, and 8 percent from charity). Of course, there were less than 3,000 families who received awards after 9/11, in contrast to Katrina's much larger number of victims.

One of the main factors used to determine the awards to the survivors of 9/11 victims was the potential lost earnings of those who were killed, many of whom worked in lucrative financial services industries. Katrina's mostly impoverished victims wouldn't get much on those same terms. But just as 9/11's victims received far more than the families of others who die tragically under less publicly traumatic circumstances, a legitimate case can be made for treating Katrina's victims much more generously than those who have been victimized by other natural disasters.

A Difficult Verification Process

Another huge challenge will be identifying those eligible for assistance. If the Republican approach to election administration is any indication, government officials will raise concerns about fraudulent claims as a justification for using excessive red-tape to make it difficult for displaced families to receive compensation. Because many of those individuals lack driver's licenses and other identification, and because other paper records like housing deeds, bills, and so forth were lost or destroyed in the disaster, the verification process will be far more difficult than it was after 9/11. In anticipation of those problems, governments at all levels should already be coordinating an effort to synthesize housing records, data from utilities, Medicaid, Medicare, Social Security, and tax agencies to make a list of people who may have been displaced. The burden should be on the government to easily enable actual victims to collect what they deserve, rather than forcing desperate people to jump through hoops.

As Brooks mentioned, the main reason why programs like Gautreaux and Moving to Opportunity haven't been emulated more widely is that residents of white middle-class neighborhoods simply don't want to live near poor black people, especially sizeable numbers of them. Providing housing subsidies much higher than the norm is the only reasonable hope for spreading the victimized families out broadly enough so that local resistance to a perceived influx doesn't reach a critical mass.

Opportunity really can arise from calamity. But seizing that opportunity requires political leadership and public sacrifice.

"Panhandlers play an important role in our society, because they are the visible face of poverty."

People Should Give Money to Panhandlers

Reggie Rivers

Panhandlers are the face of poverty, claims Reggie Rivers in the following viewpoint. According to Rivers, leaders that ask people to stop giving to panhandlers do not want to help the panhandlers but only to keep them from scaring away tourists and customers. As long as governments choose to hide rather than resolve the problems homeless beggars face, people should continue to give panhandlers money, he maintains. Rivers, a former running back for the Denver Broncos, is a talk radio host and a columnist for the Denver Post.

As you read, consider the following questions:

1. According to a Denver study cited by Rivers, how much do Denver residents give to panhandlers each year?
2. Under what conditions would it be easy to forget that homelessness is a significant issue in Denver, in the author's opinion?

Reggie Rivers, "Don't Stop Giving Change to Beggars," *Denver Post* [Colorado], August 26, 2005. Copyright 2005 the *Denver Post*. Reproduced by permission.

3. To what does Rivers compare the impulsive contributions that beggars provoke?

I give money to panhandlers. It's not part of my daily routine, but every now and then, a homeless person will be in my line of sight when I'm feeling generous, and I'll hand him or her a couple of bucks.

I don't have any expectations about how the recipient will spend the money. Maybe he'll buy food. Maybe he's saving for a bus trip to another city. Maybe he'll use the money to pay for lodging. Or maybe he'll just buy booze. It doesn't matter to me. I give him money because I can see he needs it.

Hidden Motives

[In August 2005] a study commissioned by the Downtown Denver Business Improvement District and the city's Office of Economic Development revealed that 44 percent of Denver residents are like me. Our occasional giving adds up to about $25 a year for each of us, which totals about $4.6 million a year to panhandlers.

Denver business leaders and city officials want us to stop. They say, with a straight face, that they care about panhandlers and that our impromptu donations only perpetuate the problems that beggars face. They say panhandlers need tough love if they're going to rise out of poverty. They point to the city's proposed $122 million, 10-year proposal to end homelessness, and suggest redirecting our $4.6 million a year in donations could significantly help fund this program.

With all due respect, I doubt that this study was motivated by humanitarian ideals. Business bureaus and economic development offices typically don't spend time trying to cure the complex problems of poverty, homelessness and panhandling. The objective was to figure out how to keep unattractive, malodorous, poor beggars from driving away tourists and other customers.

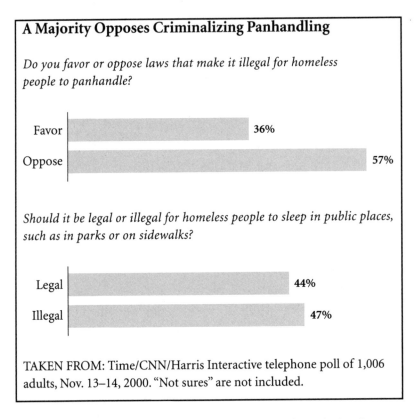

A Majority Opposes Criminalizing Panhandling

Do you favor or oppose laws that make it illegal for homeless people to panhandle?

Favor — 36%

Oppose — 57%

Should it be legal or illegal for homeless people to sleep in public places, such as in parks or on sidewalks?

Legal — 44%

Illegal — 47%

TAKEN FROM: Time/CNN/Harris Interactive telephone poll of 1,006 adults, Nov. 13–14, 2000. "Not sures" are not included.

And I imagine their concerns are well-founded. There are many people who get nervous and/or scared when they see panhandlers, and they might avoid a shop that had a lot of beggars out front. But I'm not going to stop making my occasional donations to people on street corners.

The Face of Poverty

Panhandlers play an important role in our society, because they are the visible face of poverty. The study in question focused on Denver residents, but a large percentage of middle- and upper-income families in the metro area live in suburban enclaves that are completely devoid of poverty. The tight restrictions of homeowner associations ensure that blight doesn't exist, and the cost of mortgages, HOA [home owners' association] dues, assessments and mandatory repairs make it virtually impossible to maintain a home in these neighborhoods without a substantial income.

So if you live in a poverty-free area, drive on highways crowded with your peers, work in an office building full of successful people, and never see anyone on the low end of the economy, it would be easy to forget that poor people exist and that homelessness is a significant issue in Denver.

The suggestion that our $4.6 million in donations would be better spent on other programs is true, but irrelevant. I donate money to many charities, but these impromptu donations wouldn't exist if not for panhandlers. Beggars provoke impulsive conditions in the same way that tabloids near checkout counters provoke impulse buys.

Rather than asking us to boycott panhandlers, business and city leaders should think seriously about what they can do to reduce the social problems that contribute to panhandling. I don't know how much money they spent on this survey, but if their goal was to help the poor, the money could have been better spent by donating it to a program.

If you give money to panhandlers, don't stop. They're not getting rich off your donations, but they are serving a purpose. We shouldn't push the poor out of sight; we should push them out of poverty.

> "When you give panhandlers money, you tell them that they should keep doing what they're doing for a living."

People Should Not Give Money to Panhandlers

Brad Edmonds

Giving money to panhandlers only encourages their behavior, making communities unattractive and dangerous, argues Brad Edmonds in the following viewpoint. When offered food or work, he maintains, panhandlers often refuse because they would rather beg than work. In fact, Edmonds claims, many panhandlers make a substantial living from begging. Indeed, he asserts, panhandlers use time-honored foot-in-the-door sales techniques to get people to part with their hard-earned money. Edmonds is author of There's a Government in Your Soup: Why There's Too Much Government in Your Kitchen, and What You Can Do About It.

As you read, consider the following questions:

1. According to Edmonds, why do many people remain homeless?
2. What stories does Edmonds provide to prove his assertion that the homeless are not starving?

Brad Edmonds, "The Industrious Homeless," LewRockwell.com, June 22, 2002. Reproduced by permission of the publisher and author.

3. In the author's opinion, why did people stop holding signs that say, "Will work for food"?

My [previous] article on the homeless drew a few amusing responses from readers whose experiences confirmed one of my assertions—that many, perhaps most, of those who remain homeless for any significant length of time do so because they are simply averse to work. Given the natural disutility of labor, most of us are averse to work, and fortunate indeed are those who find jobs they love, or find they can be happy in any job. Most of us recognize that we must take the bitter with the sweet, and we toil while contributing to the creation of wealth and knowledge, losing half our earned income to taxes in the process.

Keep in mind that the following stories are not the results of a scientific poll, and are not being offered as representative of the circumstances of the model homeless person. They still make for amusing reading, and learning more about these people can sharpen your wits for the next time you encounter them.

Stories of the Industrious Homeless

More than one reader informed me they'd one-upped my business card idea (I suggested that people give a Salvation Army business card to the next homeless person who wants a dollar): When approached by bums asking for money, they tried inviting the bums to lunch instead. So far, readers report that every offer has been refused, many of them rudely. This tells me that the homeless at least aren't starving. One reader observed a bum sitting on the ground, wearing a cast on his leg. At the end of the day, the bum would walk home, carrying the cast under one arm. In my own experience working in a church office, I remember one panhandler walking in with a cane. The church office was bi-level, with a set of three stairs separating the foyer from the rest of the building. I noted him using the cane to help his left leg, and struggling considerably with the stairs on the way up. As he left, he had no trouble with the stairs—he didn't use the cane or the railing—and limped on his right leg. Apparently the cane was a relatively new prop for him, and he hadn't become accustomed to using it naturally.

One reader interviewed a few panhandling bums in a medium-sized city, and found they were averaging $150 per day in handouts. Given that the $150 is "net" of deductions (indeed, there are no deductions), if that amount is won daily over 50 weeks, it comes to $37,500, or the equivalent of a salary of $62,000, assuming that only 40% is deducted from that salary. Confirmation that figures in this realm are possible is provided by another reader 1,000 miles away from the preceding one. His favorite is a four-foot-tall bum who works the same busy traffic light every day. This reader has observed the bum driving away in a "big, shiny" truck, customized with an entry ladder to accommodate his stature. The bum has been known to taunt other panhandlers at the intersection, waving wads of cash to show his success at not working.

Using Proven Techniques

Remember the "will work for food" signs? Either those didn't work—people didn't give cash—or they did work, but not as desired—perhaps people offered jobs. The short bum above holds a sign that says "please help," sending the message that he wants only cash. Apparently it works. In my fair city, bums use the foot-in-the-door technique, proven by psychologists to be effective. This technique involves asking for a small favor first, then a larger one later, the mechanism by which it works may be the suggestion to the gullible target that since the person merited the first favor, he merits the second. Our bums start by asking you the time, which not only functions as the first favor but may get you to stop while they work their way closer to you; then they ask for the dollar (incidentally, Ben Franklin used this technique: When he was lobbying for a po-

An Enabling, Not a Charitable Act

Giving money is not a charitable act. It's an act of enabling one to continue a destructive lifestyle and a tacit approval of the panhandler's conduct. Money given to panhandlers is spent immediately for drugs or alcohol. Would you want someone to give money to your son or daughter for drugs or alcohol?. . .

The entire philosophy of helping the homeless is rapidly changing, locally and nationally, from a philosophy of giving handouts with no expectations to giving a "hand up" to those who will use it to regain dignity.

Bob Holmes, Colorado Springs Gazette, *September 21, 2004.*

sition in support of an early congress, all but one member voted for Ben. Ben later borrowed a prized book from the nay-vote, and that member was a big supporter of Franklin ever after. And yes, Ben borrowed the book with that purpose in mind—read his autobiography).

Zoos tell you not to feed the animals—among other things, it teaches them to be aggressive with visitors. One reader noted the "do not feed the pigeons" signs in his city, and their analogy to the homeless. If people feed pigeons, the pigeons show up bolder and in greater numbers; they also become dependent, and—not the least of considerations—they foul the surroundings. When you give panhandlers money, you tell them that they should keep doing what they're doing for a living. You're also keeping upon the rest of us the burden of their emergency medical care, keeping them in the business of fouling your city and making it more dangerous, and maintaining their vices. It is not soft-hearted to give money to beggars, it is soft-brained and counter to the purposes of civilization. If you are doing it, stop. If you have been just saying no, you're doing the right thing. Keep it up.

Periodical Bibliography

The following articles have been selected to supplement the diverse views presented in this chapter.

Andrea Ball — "Who Is Worthy of Charity?" *American Statesman*, September 3, 2006.

Rabbi Shmuley Boteach — "Why Give Money to Beggars on the Street?" *Jerusalem Post*, September 21, 2006.

Deborah Fisk, Jaak Rakfeldt, and Erin McCormack — "Assertive Outreach: An Effective Strategy for Engaging Homeless Persons with Substance Use Disorders into Treatment," *American Journal of Drug and Alcohol Abuse*, August 2006.

The Lancet — "An SOS from Homeless People," December 3, 2005.

Los Angeles Times — "Soup Kitchen Criminals," July 29, 2006.

Maurice Martin — "Sweeping Out the Homeless Is No Answer," *People's Weekly World*, April 20, 2006.

New York Times — "Little House on the Flood Plain," September 23, 2005.

Norbert Part — "Who Is Healing the Homeless?" *Journal of Men's Health & Gender*, June 2005.

Amanda Paulson — "One City's Bold Approach to Chronic Homelessness," *Christian Science Monitor*, January 26, 2004.

Kate Quinn — "Open the Door—It's Cold Outside," *Catholic New Times*, January 4, 2004.

Gerry Roll — "How Needy Families Get Excluded from Assistance Programs," *Christian Science Monitor*, May 22, 2006.

Suzanne L. Wenzel — "Help for Homeless Women," *Washington Post*, June 16, 2006.

For Further Discussion

Chapter 1

1. Mike Rosen claims that activists exaggerate homeless estimates. The National Student Campaign Against Hunger & Homelessness (NSCAHH) in large part bases its claims that homelessness is increasing on the results of its 2004 survey of nine hundred emergency food and shelter providers. Do you think the survey might be flawed in any of the ways that Rosen suggests, or is it an adequate reflection of homelessness? Explain, citing from the texts.

2. The authors of several viewpoints in this chapter maintain that homelessness is a serious problem for a particular population of people. What do these different populations have in common and how do they differ? Do any of these similarities or differences make it more or less difficult to identify and/or help these homeless populations? Explain, citing from the viewpoints.

3. If the factors that contribute to homelessness among veterans are, as the National Coalition for Homeless Veterans suggests, a direct result of military service, how might policies designed to help this group differ from policies to help other homeless populations? Explain, citing from the viewpoints.

Chapter 2

1. Several of the authors in this chapter emphasize specific factors that they believe play a major role in homelessness. What types of evidence does each cite to support his/her/its conclusion? Which types of evidence do you find most persuasive? Explain your answers, citing from the viewpoints.

2. According to the National Coalition for the Homeless, an increase in poverty and a lack of affordable housing are the primary factors responsible for an increase in homelessness. In fact, the coalition suggests that any other contributing factors only contribute to homelessness in the context of poverty and a lack of affordable housing. Do you agree, or could some of the factors listed by the coalition and the other authors in this chapter in and of themselves lead to homelessness? Explain, citing the viewpoints.

3. Diana Mahoney contends that studies have not yet confirmed whether substance abuse causes homelessness or homelessness contributes to substance abuse among the homeless. Do any of the contributing factors cited in the other viewpoints in this chapter reveal a similarly complex relationship? Citing from the viewpoints, explain.

4. Which of the policies in chapters 3 and 4 would best address each of the factors that the authors in this chapter claim contribute to homelessness? Do any of the policies that might address one contributing factor conflict with any of the policies that might address other contributing factors? Explain why or why not, citing from the viewpoints.

Chapter 3

1. René Heybach and Patricia Nix-Hodes cite a number of international laws that identify adequate housing as a human right. Michael Tanner says, however, that affordable housing does not meet the proper definition of a right because it would interfere with the rights of others. Do you agree that a properly defined right must not conflict with the rights of others? Does your answer depend on whether the right actually does interfere or simply might interfere with the rights of others?

2. Margery Austin Turner argues that housing assistance programs improve the mobility of low-income families, helping end the cycle of poverty. Howard Husock, on the other hand, believes that housing assistance does not help low-income families but creates a cycle of dependency. Which viewpoint do you find more persuasive. Explain.

3. The chronically homeless comprise 10 percent of the homeless population but consume most of the resources devoted to homelessness. The editors of the *Christian Science Monitor* reason, therefore, that it would be more cost efficient to provide permanent housing and coordinated services to end chronic homelessness. Gloria M. Guard fears that a focus on the small percentage of chronically homeless will divert resources from families, which are the fastest growing homeless population. Do you agree with Guard that a focus on chronic homelessness will hurt homeless families? Does either viewpoint suggest a strategy that will help all homeless populations? Explain your answer, citing from the texts.

4. What commonalities among the viewpoints on each side of the debate can you find in this chapter? Explain, citing from the viewpoints.

Chapter 4

1. John Derbyshire claims that private charity, not the government, should help the homeless. Derbyshire claims that the United States was founded on the notion of self-support and quotes former president Calvin Coolidge. What major economic event(s) immediately followed Coolidge's presidency? How may those events have changed American attitudes toward the role of government in resolving community problems? Do you think those concerns are relevant today, or do you think, like Derbyshire, that private charity should resolve community problems?

2. Bruce Katz and Mark Muro believe that a housing voucher program for Hurricane Katrina victims will increase mobility and reduce poverty in New Orleans. Greg Anrig Jr. claims that because of the large number of those in need, a housing voucher subsidy would be inadequate to help low-income families escape high-poverty neighborhoods in the city. Which viewpoint do you find more persuasive? Explain, citing from the texts.

3. Reggie Rivers believes that panhandlers remind the society that poverty still exists in this country. Brad Edmonds argues that many panhandlers make a substantial living begging. What types of evidence does each author use to support his claim? Is one type of evidence more persuasive? Explain.

4. What commonalities among the viewpoints on each side of the debate can you find in this chapter? Explain, citing from the viewpoints.

Organizations to Contact

The editors have compiled the following list of organizations concerned with the issues debated in this book. The descriptions are derived from materials provided by the organizations. All have publications or information available for interested readers. The list was compiled on the date of publication of the present volume; the information provided here may change. Be aware that many organizations take several weeks or longer to respond to inquiries, so allow as much time as possible.

The American Enterprise Institute for
Public Policy Research (AEI)
1150 Seventeenth St. NW, Washington, DC   20036
(202) 862-5800 • fax: (202) 862-7178
e-mail: info@aei.org
Web site: www.aei.org

The institute is dedicated to preserving and strengthening the foundations of freedom—limited government, private enterprise, vital cultural and political institutions, and a strong foreign policy and national defense—through scholarly research, open debate, and publications. AEI research covers economics, trade, social welfare, government spending and policy, domestic politics, defense, and foreign policy. The institute publishes books, articles, reports, and its policy magazine, *American Enterprise*. Many articles, reports, and recent issues of *American Enterprise*, are available on its Web site.

Beyond Shelter
1200 Wilshire Blvd, Suite 600, Los Angeles, CA   90017
(213) 252-0772 • fax: (213) 480-0846
e-mail: info@beyondshelter.org
Web site: www.beyondshelter.org

Beyond Shelter develops and promotes programs that combat poverty, welfare dependency, and homelessness among families with children. The organization promotes housing-first initiatives because it believes that the primary cause of homelessness among families is the growing gap between housing costs and income. In addition, because shelters are unable to provide the intensive long-term assistance that homeless families require in order to stabilize their lives, Beyond Shelter seeks to increase accessibility to needed social services through service-enriched housing. On its Web site, Beyond Shelter publishes fact sheets, reports, and articles, including "Housing Plus Services: Supporting Vulnerable Families in Permanent Housing."

The Brookings Institution
1775 Massachusetts Ave. NW, Washington, DC 20036-2188
(202) 797-6000 • fax: (202) 797-6004
e-mail: brookinfo@brook.edu
Web site: www.brookings.edu

The institution is devoted to nonpartisan research, education, and publication in economics, government, foreign policy, and the social sciences. Its principal purposes are to aid in the development of sound public policies and to promote public understanding of issues of national importance. It publishes the quarterly journal the *Brookings Review*, which periodically includes articles that explore issues related to homelessness. The articles "Welfare Reform: A Mother's Work" and "Metropolitan Neighborhoods with Sheltered Homeless Populations: Evidence from the 1990 and 2000 Censuses" are available on its Web site.

Cato Institute
1000 Massachusetts Ave. NW, Washington, DC 20001-5403
(202) 842-0200 • fax: (202) 842-3490
e-mail: cato@cato.org
Web site: www.cato.org

The Cato Institute is a libertarian public policy research organization that advocates civil liberties and limited government. It has published a variety of literature concerning poverty and housing in its quarterlies the *Cato Journal* and *Regulation* and its Policy Analysis series, including the article "The Fall and Rise of Public Housing."

The Center for Law and Social Policy (CLASP)
1015 Fifteenth St. NW, Suite 400, Washington, DC 20005
(202) 906-8000 • fax: (202) 842-2885
Web site: www.clasp.org

CLASP is a national nonprofit organization that seeks to improve the economic conditions of low-income families with children. The center analyzes federal and state policies and practices in the areas of welfare reform and workforce development and produces materials designed to explain the implications of these policies and practices. Available on the CLASP Web site are numerous publications on issues related to family economic security and civil legal assistance, including "Families on the Edge: Homeless Young Parents and Their Welfare Experiences."

Children's Defense Fund (CDF)
25 E St. NW, Washington, DC 20001
(202) 628-8787
e-mail: cdfinfo@childrensdefense.org
Web site: www.childrensdefense.org

CDF works to promote the interests of children in America. It pays particular attention to the needs of poor, minority, and disabled children. Its publications include the report *Katrina's Children: A Call to Conscience and Action* and the article "Affordable Housing: A Quiet Crisis for Families with Children," which are available on its Web site.

Corporation for Supportive Housing (CSH)
50 Broadway, 17th Floor, New York, NY 10004
(212) 986-2966 • fax: (212) 986-6552
e-mail: info@csh.org
Web site: www.csh.org

CSH supports the expansion of permanent housing opportunities that are linked to comprehensive services for people with chronic health challenges such as substance abuse, mental illness, and HIV/AIDS. On its Web site, CSH has fact sheets on supportive housing needs and strategies and links to articles, including "Ending Homelessness in America: Have We Reached the Tipping Point?" and "Home Works: Solving Family Homelessness through Permanent Supportive Housing."

Homes for the Homeless (HFH)
36 Cooper Square, 6th Floor, New York, NY   10003
(212) 529-5252 • fax: (212) 529-7698
e-mail: info@homesforthehomeless.com
Web site: www.homesforthehomeless.com

HFH strives to reduce homelessness by providing families with the education and training they need to build independent lives. Participating families are housed in residential educational training centers, where they learn job, literacy, and parenting skills. Participants are also counseled on substance abuse and domestic violence. HFH publishes the reports *The New Poverty: A Generation of Homeless Families* and *Job Readiness: Crossing the Threshold from Homelessness to Employment*, which are available on its Web site.

National Alliance to End Homelessness
1518 K St. NW, Suite 206, Washington, DC   20005
(202) 638-1526 • fax: (202) 638-4664
e-mail: naeh@naeh.org
Web site: www.naeh.org

The alliance is a national organization composed of state and local nonprofit agencies, corporations, and individuals committed to the ideal that no American should have to be homeless. Its goal is to end homelessness by changing federal policy and by helping its local members serve more homeless people. Its publications include *What You Can Do to Help the Homeless* and the monthly newsletter *Alliance*.

National Coalition for Homeless Veterans (NCHV)

333-1/2 Pennsylvania Ave. SE, Washington, DC   20003
(202) 546-1969 • fax: (202) 546-2063
e-mail: nchv@nchv.org
Web site: www.nchv.org

The goal of NCHV is to end homelessness among U.S. veterans by shaping public policy and building up the capacity of service providers. A national network of community-based service providers and local, state, and federal agencies, NCHV provides emergency and supportive housing, food, health services, job training and placement assistance, legal aid, and case management support for hundreds of thousands of homeless veterans. On its Web site, NCHV publishes guides, brochures, and its monthly e-newsletter.

National Coalition for the Homeless

1012 Fourteenth St. NW, Suite 600
Washington, DC   20005-3471
(202) 737-6444 • fax: (202) 737-6445
Web site: www.nationalhomeless.org

The coalition is a national advocacy network of activists, homeless persons, service providers, and others committed to ending homelessness through public education, policy advocacy, grassroots organizing, and technical assistance. It lobbies for government programs to help the homeless, conducts research, and works as a clearinghouse on information about the homeless. In addition to many pamphlets and reports, many of which are available on its Web site, it publishes the monthly newsletter *Safety Network*.

National Student Campaign Against Hunger and Homelessness (NSCAHH)

407 S. Dearborn, Suite 701, Chicago, IL   60605
312) 291-0349 x301 • fax: (312) 275-7150
e-mail: info@studentsagainsthunger.org
Web site: www.nscahh.org

NSCAHH is a network of college and high school students, educators, and community leaders who work to fight hunger and homelessness in the United States and around the world. Its mission is to create a generation of student/community activists who will explore and understand the root causes of poverty and who will initiate positive change through service and action. It publishes the quarterly newsletter *Students Making a Difference* as well as numerous manuals, fact sheets, and handbooks, many of which are available on its Web site.

U.S. Conference of Mayors Task Force on Hunger and Homelessness
1620 Eye St. NW, 4th Floor, Washington, DC   20006
(202) 293-7330 • fax: (202) 293-2352
e-mail: info@usmayors.org
Web site: http://usmayors.org

The task force studies trends in hunger, homelessness, and community programs that address homelessness and hunger in U.S. cities. It publishes an annual report on hunger and homelessness. The current and previous years' reports are available on its Web site.

U.S. Department of Housing and Urban Development (HUD)
451 Seventh St. SW, Washington, DC   20410
(202) 708-1112
Web site: http://www.hud.gov/homeless/index.cfm

HUD promotes cooperation among federal agencies on homelessness issues. On the "Homeless" page of its Web site, HUD provides links to state and local resources for those who are homeless. It also provides information on national and HUD assistance programs for service providers and links to homeless organizations. Materials on issues concerning the homeless are accessible in its online library.

Bibliography of Books

Cynthia J. Bogard   *Seasons Such as These: How Home-lessness Took Shape in America.* New York: Aldine de Gruyter, 2003.

Kurt Borchard   *The Word on the Street: Homeless Men in Las Vegas.* Reno: University of Nevada Press, 2005.

Rachel G. Bratt, Michael E. Stone, and Chester Hartman, eds.   *A Right to Housing: Foundation for a New Social Agenda.* Philadelphia: Temple University Press, 2006.

Judith Lynn Failer   *Who Qualifies for Rights? Homelessness, Mental Illness, and Civil Commitment.* Ithaca, NY: Cornell University Press, 2002.

Leonard C. Feldman   *Citizens Without Shelter: Homelessness, Democracy, and Political Exclusion.* Ithaca, NY: Cornell University Press, 2004.

Marni Finkelstein   *With No Direction Home: Homeless Youth on the Road and in the Streets.* Belmont, CA: Thomson/Wadsworth, 2005.

Lisa K. Foster and Patricia Snowdon   *Addressing Long-Term Homelessness: Permanent Supportive Housing.* Sacramento: California State Library, California Research Bureau, 2003.

Kim Hopper   *Reckoning with Homelessness.* Ithaca, NY: Cornell University Press, 2003.

Christopher Jencks — *The Homeless.* Cambridge, MA: Harvard University Press, 1994.

Jeff Karabanow — *Being Young and Homeless: Understanding How Youth Enter and Exit Street Life.* New York: Peter Lang, 2004.

Michelle Kennedy — *Without a Net: Middle Class and Homeless (with Kids) in America: My Story.* New York: Viking, 2005.

Ken Kyle — *Contextualizing Homelessness: Critical Theory, Homelessness, and Federal Policy Addressing the Homeless.* New York: Routledge, 2005.

Anthony Marcus — *Where Have All the Homeless Gone? The Making and Unmaking of a Crisis.* New York: Berghahn Books, 2006.

Marjorie Mayers — *Street Kids and Streetscapes: Panhandling, Politics and Prophecies.* New York: Peter Lang, 2001.

Paul Milbourne and Paul Cloke, eds. — *International Perspective on Rural Homelessness.* New York: Routledge, 2006.

Don Mitchell — *The Right to the City: Social Justice and the Fight for Public Space.* New York: Guilford, 2003.

Frank Munger, ed. — *Laboring Below the Line: The New Ethnography of Poverty, Low-Wage Work, and Survival in the Global Economy.* New York: Russell Sage Foundation, 2002.

Robert S. Ogilvie — *Voluntarism, Community Life, and the American Ethic.* Bloomington: Indiana University Press, 2004.

D. Wayne Osgood, E. Michael Foster, Constance Flanagan, and Gretchen R. Ruth, eds. — *On Your Own Without a Net: The Transition to Adulthood for Vulnerable Populations.* Chicago: University of Chicago Press, 2005.

Paul A. Rollinson and John T. Pardeck — *Homelessness in Rural America: Policy and Practice.* New York: Haworth, 2006.

Michael S. Scott — *Panhandling.* Washington, DC: U.S. Dept. of Justice, Office of Community Oriented Policing Services, 2002.

Natasha Slesnick — *Our Runaway and Homeless Youth: A Guide to Understanding.* Westport, CT: Praeger, 2004.

Jean Calterone Williams — *"A Roof over My Head": Homeless Women and the Shelter Industry.* Boulder: University Press of Colorado, 2003.

Mary E. Williams, ed. — *Poverty and the Homeless.* San Diego: Greenhaven, 2004.

Michael Yankoski — *Under the Overpass.* Sisters, OR: Multnomah, 2005.

Index

A

Access to Community Care and Affective Services and Supports (ACCESS), 85
Addiction disorders, 72–73, 74–78
Adolescents, benefits of voucher programs for, 122, 124
Affordable housing
   funding of, 24
   lack of, 65, 68–71
   See also Housing vouchers
Aid to Families with Dependent Children (AFDC), 66, 102
Alcohol addiction, 72–73, 74–78
Ali Forney Center, 56–57
Alioto, Angela, 48
Alliance to End Homelessness, 107–108
American Civil Liberties Union Foundation, 88
American Enterprise Institute for Public Policy Research (AEI), 187
Anderson, Jim, 134
Anrig, Greg, Jr., 169
Archibold, Randal C., 30
Assertive community treatment, 84, 86
Assistance programs
   for emancipated foster children, 45–52
   See also Housing assistance programs

B

Bailey, Darnell, 45–47, 50–52
Beyond Shelter, 107, 187–188
Bringing America Home Act, 16

Brookings Institution, The, 188
Brooks, David, 170, 173
Bush administration
   budget policies of, 99
   homelessness initiatives of, 151–157
   housing program legislation of, 125–128

C

Carson, Julia, 16
Caruso, Laura M., 108
Case managers, 84
Cash payments, to indigents, 160–162
Cato Institute, 188–189
Center for Law and Social Policy (CLASP), 189
Cherin, Rebecca, 48
Chicago Coalition for the Homeless (CCH), 62, 111
Children
   benefits of voucher programs for, 122
   effects of homelessness on, 19–20
   foster, 44–52
   in poverty, 67
   school issues of homeless, 20
   See also Homeless families
Children's Defense Fund (CDF), 189
Christian Science Monitor, 138
Chronic homelessness
   defining, 29
   efforts to end, 16, 87
   focusing on, hurts homeless families, 142–146

government initiatives to reduce, 151–157

housing strategies for, 153–
154

mental illness and, 81

permanent housing will reduce, 138–141

City ordinances, 149–150

Civil War veterans, 95

Clines, Francis X., 100

Clinton, Hilary, 130

Coalition for the Homeless, 93

Committee on Economic, Social
and Cultural Rights, 112–114

Community Mental Health Centers Act, 163

Community Partnership to End
Homelessness Act, 143–146

Coolidge, Calvin, 162–163

Corporation for Supportive Housing (CSH), 189–190

Critical Time Intervention, 85

D

da Costa Nuñez, Ralph, 108

Dayton (OH), 139–140

Deinstitutionalization, 163

Denver, 175–177

Department of Housing and Ur-
ban Development (HUD). See
U.S. Department of Housing and
Urban Development (HUD)

Department of Veterans Affairs
(VA), 43, 97

Dependency, created by housing
vouchers, 130–134

Derbyshire, John, 158

Desert Storm veterans, 97

Discharge planning, 86

Discrimination
housing, 89–90, 92
against the mentally ill, 83

Domestic violence, 72, 88–92

Donahue, Maggie, 49–50

Drug abuse, 72–73, 74–78

Drum, Kevin, 171

Duerr-Berrick, Jill, 49

E

Economic problems contributing
to homelessness, 64–65, 101–102

Edmonds, Brad, 178

Eighth Amendment, 150

Emergency shelters. See Homeless
shelters

Employed persons, homeless, 65–
66, 100–104

Employer-sponsored health insurance, 62

Employment opportunities
lack of, 64–66
voucher programs and selection of, 124–125

Engel, Mark, 135–136

Espinoza, Sandi, 33, 35

Evictions, 90

F

Fagan, Kevin, 44

Federal Emergency Relief Administration, 15

First Amendment, 150

Fischer, Will, 166

Food banks, growing number of,
22–23

Foster children
chronic homelessness and, 81
homelessness is serious problem among, 44–52

Free speech, 150

G

Gautreaux demonstration, 122–125, 170–171
Gay youths, homelessness is serious problem among, 53–58
General Assistance (GA) benefits, 68
Government funding
  cuts in, 23–24, 66–68, 103–104
  of health care, 62
  of homeless programs, 35
  of housing assistance programs, 103–104
  of mental health programs, 87
  reduced, for homeless families, 143–146
Government policies, 15–16
Government programs
  can reduce homelessness, 151–157
  during Depression, 15
  housing assistance programs, 70–71
  integrative service programs, 83–87
  will not reduce homelessness, 158–163
  See also Housing assistance programs; Welfare programs
Great Depression, 14–15, 95
Greyhound therapy, 32
Guard, Gloria, 142
Gulf War veterans, 97

H

Haddow, Donna, 35
Harvard Mental Health Letter, 79
Haven of Hope, 34
Health care insurance, lack of, 61–62, 67, 71

Health problems, of homeless children, 19–20
Heybach, René, 110
High-poverty neighborhoods, 120–122
Holguin, Brenda, 34
Holmes, Bob, 181
Homeless families
  domestic violence and, 88–92
  lack of public assistance and, 67
  more programs are needed for, 142–146
  positive characteristics of, 20
  problems faced by, 108
  services for, 20
  See also Children
Homeless mothers
  single, 134–135
  working, 103
  See also Homeless families
Homeless population
  accurate number of, 27–28
  changing nature of, 19
  characteristics of, 69
  diversity of, 16
  local ordinances affecting, 149–150
Homeless shelters
  demand for, 24–25, 101
  enhanced services by, 108
  failures of, 107
  funding of, 16, 23–24
  for LGBT youths, 56–57
  number of, 23
  problems for gay youth at, 55
Homeless veterans, 37–43, 93–99
Homelessness
  among gay youths, 53–58
  attitudes toward, 14–17
  costs of, 86
  criminalization of, 149–150

defining, 28–29, 134–135
domestic violence and, 88–92
factors contributing to, 63–73
foster care and, 47, 81
government initiatives will reduce, 151–157
government initiatives will not reduce, 158–163
is exaggerated problem, 26–29
is widespread problem, 21–25
lack of affordable health care and, 61–62, 68–71
lack of affordable housing and, 68–71
mental illness and, 72, 79–87, 163
policies concerning, 14–17
poverty and, 64–68
preventing, 154–156
rural, 30–36
welfare reform increases, 100–104
Homes for the Homeless (HFH), 190
Housing
is a human right, 110–115
is not a human right, 116–118
permanent, 138–141
Housing assistance programs
cost-effective, 153–154
cuts in, 103–104
mentally ill and, 81–83, 87
need for, 70–71
for veterans, 97–99
See also Housing vouchers
Housing discrimination, against battered women, 89–90, 92
Housing problems, 65, 68–71
Housing vouchers
are inadequate for Hurricane Katrina victims, 169–173
benefits of, 119–128
cuts in, 103–104

legislation affecting, 125–128
problems with, 129–137
promote dependency, 130–134
will help Hurricane Katrina victims, 164–168
Housing-first programs
debate over, 107–109
will reduce chronic homelessness, 138–141
HUD. See U.S. Department of Housing and Urban Development (HUD)
Human rights
housing as, 110–115
housing is not one of, 116–118
nature of, 117–118
Hurricane Katrina victims
housing vouchers are inadequate for, 169–173
housing vouchers will help, 164–168
Husock, Howard, 129

I

Incarceration, 81
Income disparities, 66
Injured servicemembers, 39–42
Integrated Services for Homeless Adults with Serious Mental Illness, 85
Integrative service programs, 83–87
Interagency Council on Homelessness (ICH), 139–140, 151–157
International Convention on the Elimination of All Forms of Racial Discrimination, 111–112
International Covenant on Civil and Political Rights, 111

International Covenant on Economic, Social, and Cultural Rights (ICESCR), 111, 112
Iraq veterans, 40–42, 98

J

Jencks, Christopher, 15
Joblessness, 102–103

K

Katz, Bruce, 164
Kennelly, Theresa, 140
Knight, Katrina, 101
Kusmer, Kenenth, 95, 96

L

Larkin Extended Aftercare for Supported Emancipation Program (LEASE), 45–52
L.C., Olmstead v., 86
Leuhrs, Tom, 28
Lobato, John, 31–32, 34
Local ordinances, 149–150
Loitering laws, 149
Loper v. New York City Police Dept., 150
Low Income Housing Tax Credit (LIHTC), 121
Low-income housing, concentrated, 120–121

M

Mahoney, Diana, 74
Mangano, Philip, 32, 140, 151
Manic-depressives, untreated, 84
Marks, Alexandra, 40
Mauck, James, 144
McKinney-Vento Homeless Assistance Act, 15, 24, 143

Medicaid, 67, 86, 87
Mental illness, 72, 79–87, 163
Minimum wage, erosion of value of, 65, 103
Mok, Frank, 53
Moving to Opportunity (MTO) program, 122–125, 170–171
Muro, Mark, 164

N

National Alliance to End Homelessness, 190
National Coalition for Homeless Veterans (NCHV), 37, 191
National Coalition for the Homeless (NCH), 63, 191
National Coalition on Homelessness, 35
National Student Campaign Against Hunger & Homelessness, 21, 191–192
Nelson, Cary T., 34
New Freedom Commission on Mental Health, 87
New York City, homeless youth population in, 54
New York City Housing Authority (NYCHA), 131–135
New York City Police Dept., Loper v., 150
Nix-Hodes, Patricia, 110

O

Olmstead v. L.C., 86
Ononvakpuri, Ulili, 50–51
Outreach programs, 84

P

Panhandlers
people should give to, 174–177

people should not give to, 178–181

Panhandling laws, 149, 150

Parvensky, John, 31

Payne, James L., 161

People with disabilities, 68

Permanent housing will reduce chronic homelessness, 138–141

Personal Responsibility and Work Opportunity Reconciliation Act, 66

Pollio, David E., 76

Post, Patricia A., 33

Post traumatic stress disorders (PTSDs), 38–39, 97

Poverty
  concentrated, 120–122
  declining public assistance and, 66–68
  domestic violence and, 90–91
  homelessness and, 64–68
  lack of work opportunities and, 64–66

Prevention programs, for homelessness, 154–156

Psychiatric hospitals, discharge planning from, 86

Psychiatric illness. See Mental illness

Psychiatric treatment, 83

Public assistance. See Housing assistance programs; Welfare programs

Public spaces, vagrancy in, 159–160

R

Rainey, Amy, 56

Rector, Robert, 15

Reed, Jack, 144

Rent subsidy vouchers. See Housing vouchers

Revolutionary War, 95

Rhorer, Trent, 150

Risk factors, for homelessness
  addiction disorders, 72–73, 74–78
  domestic violence, 72, 88–92
  housing problems, 68–71
  lack of affordable health care, 61–62, 68–71
  mental illness, 72, 79–87
  poverty, 64–68

Rivers, Reggie, 174

Roman, Nan, 16, 47, 155

Roosevelt, Franklin D., 15

Rosen, Mike, 26

Rural homelessness
  is serious problem, 30–36
  solutions to, 33–36

Rutkowski, Ed, 133

S

Said, Barbara, 166

Samaritan Initiative, 16, 152–154

San Francisco, 149–150, 159–162

Schizophrenics, untreated, 84

School difficulties, of homeless children, 20

Schools, voucher programs and selection of, 123–124

Seattle, Washington, 149

Section 8 housing, 24, 103–104, 129–137, 167
  See also Housing vouchers

September 11th Victims Compensation Fund, 171–172

Sex work, among gay youths, 57

Shelters. See Homeless shelters

Single mothers, 134–135

Sinkin, Gerald, 28

Sinkin, Natalie, 28

Snyder, Mitch, 15, 27

Social programs, cuts in funding of, 23–24

Social Security Disability Insurance (SSDI), 83

State and Local Housing Flexibility Act, 125–128

Stoops, Michael, 35

Substance abuse, 72–78

Supplemental Security Income (SSI), 68, 83

Supported employment, 86

Supported housing, 82

Supportive housing, 82, 87, 153–154

Swick, Kevin J., 20

Swope, Christopher, 133

T

Tanner, Michael, 116

Tax credits, 121, 166

Temporary Assistance to Needy Families (TANF), 66

10-Year Plans, 156–157

Transitional housing units, 34, 82

Treatment programs, 83–84

Turner, Margery Austin, 119

Turner, Vanessa, 41–42

U

Unemployment rates, 64–65

Uninsured Americans, 61–62

United Nations, 111, 112–114

U.S. Conference of Mayors Task Force on Hunger and Homelessness, 192

U.S. Department of Housing and Urban Development (HUD), 35, 69–70, 71, 165–166, 192

See also Section 8 housing

United States, growth of homelessness in, 22–25

U.S. military actions, as contributing to homelessness, 93–99

Universal Declaration of Human Rights, 111

V

VA (Veterans Affairs) disability benefits, 97–98

Vagabonds, 94–95

Vagrancy, 95

Vanderslice, Becky, 34, 36

Varick, Richard, 95

Veterans

disability benefits for, 97–98

homeless, 37–43, 93–99

housing assistance for, 97–99

injured, 39–42

Vietnam veterans, 96–97

Voucher programs. *See* Housing vouchers

Voucher recipients

creating dependency in, 130–134

as problem tenants, 135–137

W

Wage levels, declining, 65, 102–103

War, as contributing to homelessness, 93–99

Wealth disparities, 66

Welfare programs

cuts in, 66–68

reforms to, 66, 100–104

Wolfe, Phyllis, 47

Women

domestic violence and, 88–92

See also Homeless mothers

Work opportunities
  lack of, 64–66
  voucher programs and selection of, 124–125
Working homeless, 65–66, 100–104

Works Progress Administration, 15
World War II, 15, 95–96
World War I veterans, 95